Open for Debate

Racial Profiling

Open for Debate

Racial Profiling

Deborah Kops

Marshall Cavendish
Benchmark
New York

For John

With thanks to Darin Frederickson,
Phoenix Police Department detective,
for his expert review of this manuscript.

Marshall Cavendish Benchmark
99 White Plains Road
Tarrytown, NY 10591-9001
www.marshallcavendish.us

Library of Congress Cataloging-in-Publication Data
Kops, Deborah.
Racial profiling / by Deborah Kops.
p. cm. — (Open for debate)
Summary: "Focuses on the debate surrounding racial profiling in the United States—
including a historical look at criminal profiles and U.S. government initiatives like
Japanese-American internment during WWII through to the modern anti-terrorist age—
through scholarly opinions, statistics, and studies"—Provided by publisher.
Includes bibliographical references and index.
ISBN-13: 978-0-7614-2298-3
ISBN-10: 0-7614-2298-6
1. Racial profiling in law enforcement—United States—Juvenile literature.
2. Japanese Americans—Evacuation and relocation, 1942-1945—Juvenile fiction.
3. War on Terrorism, 2001—Juvenile literature. 4. Crime and race—United States—Juvenile literature. I.
Title. II. Series.
HV8141.K677 2006
363.2'308900973—dc22
2005037064

Photo research by Linda Sykes Picture Research, Inc., Hilton Head, SC

AP/Wide World Photos: cover, 1, 2–3, 5, 6, 28, 42, 53, 74, 81, 85, 104;
Bettmann/ Corbis: 15, 22, 34, 69; Bettmann/Corbis: 22. 34. 69; Soqui Ted/Corbis Sygma: 64;
Chip East/Reuters/Corbis: 89; Peter Dench/Corbis: 91.

Editorial Director: Michelle Bisson
Art Director: Anahid Hamparian
Series Designer: Sonia Chaghatzbanian

Printed in China
1 3 5 6 4 2

Contents

FELIX MORKA, ON THE LEFT, AND HIS LAWYERS REVIEW A VIDEOTAPE OF NEW JERSEY STATE POLICEMEN DURING A TRAFFIC STOP. MORKA, AN INTERNATIONAL HUMAN RIGHTS LAWYER, WAS ONE OF THE MINORITY DRIVERS WHO TESTIFIED ON APRIL 9, 2001, DURING THE U.S. SENATE JUDICIARY COMMITTEE'S HEARINGS ON RACIAL PROFILING.

Introduction

On March 30, 2000, a committee of the U. S. Senate listened quietly to the testimony of Master Sergeant Rossano Gerald, of the U. S. Army. The sergeant, who is African American, told the committee members about an incident that had occurred two years before on an Oklahoma highway. On a hot summer's day, he was driving to a family reunion from his army base in Maryland with his twelve-year-old son, Gregory.

"As soon as we crossed the border from Arkansas," he said, "I noticed patrol cars in the area and began driving even more carefully than usual." Within a few minutes, a highway state trooper signaled for him to pull over despite his extra careful driving. The trooper scolded Sergeant Gerald for following the car in front of him too closely, and let him go. But soon another trooper pulled the sergeant over, and their encounter was much more painful for him and his son Gregory.

This trooper, who was called Trooper Perry, accused Sergeant Gerald of changing lanes without signaling, which the army officer said was not true. After the trooper wrote up a warning, which is not as serious as a traffic ticket, he asked the sergeant if he could search his car. He had just made a drug bust, or arrest, and he was looking for more cars with drugs. Sergeant Gerald refused to have his car searched, but legally, Trooper Perry could search the outside of the car without the sergeant's consent. By then, a second patrol car had pulled over.

"Trooper Perry called for the K-9 unit from the second patrol car," Sergeant Gerald explained to the committee. ("K-9" is shorthand for canine, meaning a dog.) A trooper walked the dog around the sergeant's car. According to the sergeant, the dog did not alert—he did not bark, whimper, or give a sign that he had discovered anything. The trooper claimed that it did, and this gave him the legal right to search the inside of the officer's car.

The trooper asked the army sergeant and his son to get in his patrol car. Then he returned to the sergeant's car. He drilled beneath the carpet and accused Sergeant Gerald of having a secret compartment. It was actually a footrest that came with the car. The trooper did not seem to believe the army sergeant. He handcuffed him, and another trooper took his son Gregory into the car with the dog to question him. The dog barked continuously at the boy, who was afraid of being bitten.

After two hours of searching and questioning, Trooper Perry had found no evidence that Sergeant Gerald was carrying any drugs and let him go. The damages he had made to the sergeant's car cost over $1,000 to fix. The real damages, however, were much more difficult to repair. They were psychological.

"This experience was very traumatic for Gregory," the sergeant told the senators. "Throughout the interrogation, he was frightened and crying."

The army officer felt humiliated himself. "I was ashamed that people driving by would think I had committed a serious crime," he said. "It was particularly hard to be treated like a criminal in front of my impressionable young son. . . . I served our country in Somalia and in the Gulf War. I don't want my son to think that this kind of behavior [from] anyone in uniform is acceptable. I hope that coming forward to tell my story might prevent other people of color from being treated this way."

What Is Racial Profiling?

Sergeant Gerald's story interested the Senate committee because they were conducting a hearing on racial profiling. In the past year there had been about a thousand articles in the nation's newspapers touching on the issue of whether minority groups were being singled out by law enforcement agents. Many people seemed to believe this was true. The Senate was trying to determine whether Sergeant Gerald's case was an example of a growing national problem.

Racial profiling is a method that police and other law enforcement agents use to catch someone who has committed a crime or is about to commit one. It is a controversial method. In fact, even the meaning of racial profiling is controversial.

Some people think the term means that a police officer stops someone for questioning or for a search because of his or her race. That is the narrower definition. According to a broader definition, a police officer who uses racial profiling decides to question someone on the basis of several factors, including race. Other factors that might influence him are the person's age and style of dress, the type of neighborhood, and the time of day.

If we use this broad definition of racial profiling, the practice is much more common among law enforcement officials than if we were to use the narrower, more limited one. In this book, we will use that broad definition, which most scholars recommend, including Randall Kennedy, a respected legal authority on the subject. As Kennedy wrote: "Properly understood . . . racial profiling occurs whenever police routinely use race as a negative signal that, along with an accumulation of other signals, causes an officer to react with suspicion."

Why Many Law Enforcement Officials Use Racial Profiling

The main reason that police officers, both white and African American, use racial profiling is because a disproportionate number of African Americans and other minorities commit crimes. For example, between 1992 and 1996, blacks were about 12 percent of the population. During that time, 58 percent of all carjackers, who steal automobiles by threatening the driver, were African American.

Although there is no simple explanation for why a disproportionate number of blacks commit crimes, one important reason is economic. In 2000, 18 percent of blacks were living below the U.S. poverty line. According to a study conducted in 2004, almost half of the black men living in New York City had no jobs. Police and other law enforcement agents do not focus on society's social problems. They concentrate on making sure people obey the law. A substantial number think racial profiling is a logical technique for crime prevention.

The High Cost of Racial Profiling

Many people object to racial profiling because they think it discriminates against blacks and other minorities. The American Civil Liberties Union in New Jersey denounced it as part of the United States' sad history of racism, which has included the segregation, or separation, of whites and blacks in schools and other public places. "Racial profiling was born of slavery, raised by segregation, and has matured under pervasive, patently false stereotypes of minorities, especially African Americans and Latinos," the organization declared.

Kennedy has argued that the humiliation that racial profiling causes innocent blacks is too high a cost to pay for what may appear to be an efficient tool of law enforcement. Although Sergeant Gerald's experience was an extreme example of what it is like for an innocent black person to be pulled over by a police officer, the experience is never pleasant. For some black people it is replayed again and again.

Those who are repeatedly and wrongfully profiled, Kennedy cautions, may eventually develop a very negative attitude toward police officers, judges, and others who represent the law. "Racial profiling constantly adds to the sense of resentment felt by blacks of every social stratum toward the law enforcement establishment," he wrote. "Ironically," he added, "this is a cost of racial profiling that may well hamper law enforcement."

Racial Profiling Remains a National Issue

Although most Americans weren't aware of Sergeant Gerald's testimony before the Senate committee, many had heard about more famous African Americans who had been stopped on the nation's highways. Some, like Wesley Snipes, were actors. Others were athletes, including the track and field Olympic gold medalist Al Joyner and the basketball star Jamaal Wilkes. They hadn't stolen a car and they weren't driving under the influence of alcohol. It was becoming painfully clear why so many African Americans were being stopped. Their offense, described with cynical humor, was that they were "driving while black."

During the presidential election of 2000, Al Gore, the Democratic candidate, and George W. Bush, his Republican opponent, made it clear that they opposed racial profiling just like, it seemed, most Americans. A year later, though, the issue was suddenly more complicated, and many who had condemned racial profiling were rethinking their position.

On September 11, 2001, nineteen Muslim Arab men hijacked four commercial American jets. The men flew three of the planes they had commandeered into the twin towers of the World Trade Center and into the Pentagon. The fourth plane crashed in a field in Pennsylvania after some passengers overpowered the hijackers. It was meant to fly into the White House or the U.S. Capitol.

Since that tragic day when almost three thousand people were killed, U.S. law enforcement officials have been on the lookout for terrorists who are trying to enter the country or are already in it and planning to do harm. Should airport screeners randomly pull people out of line who are waiting for a quick security check in order to question them and search them more thoroughly, or should they focus on Arab passengers? What about in subways, where a potential suicide bomber may be boarding a train? So far no U.S. city supports routinely profiling an ethnic group in order to find terrorists. Neither does the nation's Transportation Security Administration, which establishes the procedures followed by airport screeners. But some Americans wish they would.

On July 7, 2005, four suicide bombers killed fifty-six people on London's subways and on a double decker bus. Weeks later, New York City's mayor Michael Bloomberg announced that police officers would begin randomly checking the bags of subway riders. There weren't many complaints over the bag searches, but some objected loudly that they would be random. Why not just focus on young men from the Middle East or from South Asia, where there are many small terrorist groups? If a police officer did so, he would be singling out these young men because of their ethnic, rather than racial, background.

The debate over racial profiling has become a debate over racial and ethnic profiling, and it isn't going to go away anytime soon. Those who support this type of profiling believe that it is the most effective way to fight crime, including terrorism. Many who object to racial and ethnic profiling believe that it threatens some of the nation's most cherished ideals. They believe it goes against the rights of Americans that are protected by the Constitution, including freedom from racial discrimination. Profiling also seems to contradict an image of the United States that Americans hold dear: For centuries the country has been a haven for immigrants from every corner of the globe, including Arab countries, who have come looking for a better life.

The possibility of a new wave of ethnic profiling directed at Arab Americans troubles members of another ethnic group: Japanese Americans. Some of them remember a painful period that they and their families endured during World War II. After the Japanese bombed an American military base at Pearl Harbor, in Hawaii, more than 110,000 Japanese Americans paid a heavy price. The American government was afraid that some of them might be spying for Japan, and forced them to leave their homes on the West Coast and live in temporary internment camps for almost four years.

Ruth Okimoto, who had lived in one of the internment camps as a child, commented, "Under certain circumstances, I think what happened to the Japanese Americans can happen to any group. We see part of that jingoism and patriotism today. . . . It's true that if you don't remember the past, . . . you repeat the mistakes of the past. And I think the Japanese Americans almost have a duty to step forward and make sure that it doesn't happen to another ethnic group."

1
Looking Like the Enemy: The Internment of Japanese Americans during World War II

Back in 1942, when President Franklin Delano Roosevelt (FDR) signed Executive Order 9066, no one had heard of the terms racial or ethnic profiling. But that order forced about 110,000 men, women, and children to leave their homes because they were Japanese or Japanese American.

Kinya Noguchi remembers the moment he learned that he would have to leave his home on the West Coast, where his family farmed. He was in seventh grade. "All through the seven years of school we were taught that individuals had their rights and everybody was equal. And here this order comes out saying that we had to move out. The crops were doing so well. And we thought finally the crops would produce enough so that we can have a little money. . . . So I was on my hands and knees pulling the weeds. When that executive order came out, I dropped my little shovel and I ran home. I was devastated."

Frank H. Wu, dean of Wayne State University Law School, sees connections between this episode in American

THIS FAMILY IS LEAVING HOME FOR AN INTERNMENT CAMP. IN 1942, ABOUT 110,000 JAPANESE AMERICANS LIVING IN CALIFORNIA WERE FORCED TO LIVE IN THESE CAMPS. THE U.S. GOVERNMENT BELIEVED THEY WERE A SECURITY RISK AND MIGHT BE TEMPTED TO SPY FOR JAPAN DURING WORLD WAR II, DESPITE A TOTAL LACK OF EVIDENCE OF DISLOYALTY.

history, which followed Japan's bombing of Pearl Harbor, and the increasing support in the United States for racial and ethnic profiling after the terrorist attacks on the World Trade Center and the Pentagon. "The internment of Japanese Americans during World War II," he said, "is the obvious precedent for the treatment of Arab Americans and Muslim Americans in the aftermath of September 11, 2001, terrorist attacks."

The Attack on Pearl Harbor

The events that led to the internment of Japanese Americans began in the 1930s. At that time, there was a worldwide depression. Unemployment was rising around the world, and trade between nations was declining. The economic hardships that so many were experiencing made people eager for change, and this made it easier for aggressive leaders to come into power. Germany was ruled by Adolf Hitler, a military dictator who built a large army. In Italy another dictator, Benito Mussolini, was in power.

In Asia, Japan pursued a very aggressive strategy in order to improve its economy. In 1931 it invaded Manchuria, in northern China. By 1937 Japan and China were involved in a full-scale war. One year later, Japan controlled most of China. The United States was alarmed by this display of Japanese aggression, which closed off United States trade with China, but the nation was more concerned with the events unfolding in Europe.

On September 1, 1939, Hitler's army invaded Poland. France and Great Britain were Poland's allies, and two days later they declared war against Germany. The German army seemed unstoppable; by June 1940 Hitler had conquered Denmark, Norway, Holland, Belgium, and France. It began attacking Great Britain next.

Meanwhile, the tensions between the United States and Japan were growing more intense. In September 1940, Japan joined forces with Germany and Italy; they became known as the Axis powers. The United States retaliated. President Roosevelt announced the United States would no longer ship aviation fuel or scrap metal to Japan, which badly needed both for its army. After Japan invaded French Indochina in the summer of 1941, the United States ended all trade with Japan.

On December 7, 1941, Japanese aircraft carriers decorated with red suns—like the Japanese flag—flew across 3,000 miles of the Pacific Ocean and attacked the U.S. naval base in Pearl Harbor, in Hawaii. Eight battleships were sunk or damaged and more than 2,400 people were killed. The next day, the United States declared war against Japan. The wars in Europe and Asia had become a global war—World War II.

The U.S. Government Worries about Spies

After the attack on Pearl Harbor, the U.S. government rounded up more than 1,500 Japanese whom it decided were "dangerous aliens." (An alien is a foreigner who has not become a citizen.) The Justice Department took charge of them and held them in alien detention camps for months and sometimes years.

John Tateishi, who belongs to the National Japanese American Citizens League, remembered those days after the attack. "Immediately after Pearl Harbor, the FBI [Federal Bureau of Investigation] swept through our communities, arrested our leaders and elders, and held them in indefinite detention, not releasing any information."

In addition to these so-called dangerous aliens, the U.S. government was worried about citizens who might feel some loyalty toward its enemies and be willing to spy for them. The government was particularly worried about Japanese Americans—people born in the United States to Japanese parents. A few months before the attack on Pearl Harbor, U.S. intelligence agents—who gathered information about the enemy— learned that Japan had established a network of spies in the United States. After the attack, intelligence agents continued to warn the government that there were spies working inside the country.

U.S. military leaders were most concerned about any

spies on the West Coast, where most Japanese Americans lived. In the region were important army and navy centers, aircraft factories, and shipyards that would make good targets for the enemy. Canada, an ally fighting with the United States against the Axis powers, had similar worries and began moving over 20,000 people of Japanese ancestry, many of whom were Canadian-born citizens, away from Canada's west coast.

The United States was not ready to take such a drastic action. It had a much larger population of ethnic Japanese—those born in Japan who were not already in detention centers, and those born in the United States to Japanese parents. Instead it began to supervise ethnic Japanese on the West Coast. There were dawn-to-dusk curfews and restrictions on travel. A Japanese American living in California had to ask permission to drive more than five miles from home. A truck farmer needed permission to take his vegetables on a delivery route. Even an appointment to see a dentist became complicated. One woman later wrote that she was unable to get permission in time to visit her dying mother, who lived in another town in Oregon.

When the U.S. government imposed these restrictions, it did not make a distinction between those who were citizens and those who weren't. Everyone of Japanese ancestry was treated the same way except for the "dangerous aliens." The same restrictions were not applied, however, to U.S. citizens who had German or Italian parents or ancestors, even though the United States was at war with those countries, too.

While the War Department debated a larger plan of action, Americans' fears and prejudices sometimes got out of control. People accused ethnic Japanese of lacing the produce they grew with poison before shipping it to the market. In Hawaii, where a third of the people had Japanese ancestors, ethnic Japanese were accused of planting their crops so that they pointed toward bombing targets, which Japan's bomber pilots would see from the sky.

In California, children who looked Japanese worried about their safety. When they were on their way to school, some people threw rocks at them or spat at them and called them names. Toru Saito recalled, "I was playing out on the street with my brother and someone called me a Jap . . . and I didn't know what it meant. I asked my mother, and my mother was ashamed and reluctant to tell me."

U.S. intelligence agents continued to sound the alarm about Japanese spy networks on the West Coast. The country's War Department recommended a similar approach to that of Canada. The department wanted to establish exclusion zones. The zones would surround areas that were of strategic importance to the United States, such as military installations and ports. Their goal was to remove ethnic Japanese.

On February 19, 1942, President Roosevelt signed Executive Order 9066, which outlined the War Department's plan. Congress approved it a month later. Although there were some exclusion zones on the East Coast, most were near the Pacific Ocean.

Roosevelt's executive order did not mention that ethnic Japanese in particular would have to leave these sensitive zones, but everyone in the War Department and the Army understood that they were the focus of the order. Very few politicians or organizations defended the right of ethnic Japanese to remain in their homes. The highly respected American Friends Service Committee (AFSC), a Quaker organization, was a notable exception and spoke up for ethnic Japanese. Clarence Pickett, the organization's executive secretary, encouraged AFSC members to help "reduce the force of this calamity, which has come upon the Japanese population."

Ethnic Japanese Leave Their Homes

Leaving their homes was a painful experience for ethnic Japanese. They were given at most two weeks' notice to pack up their things. But they had to give away most of their belongings because they could only bring with them whatever they could carry in their hands. They abandoned houses and businesses that had taken years of hard work to acquire. Vegetables were left to rot in the fields. A total of about 110,000 people were evacuated.

At first, the ethnic Japanese gathered in assembly centers. Some were fairgrounds or racetracks that had quickly been converted into camps. The most unlucky families had to stay in smelly horse barns. Others lived in military-style barracks. All were surrounded by barbed wire fences and supervised by armed guards.

In late summer and early fall of 1942, the people living in the assembly centers boarded trains that took them to more permanent living quarters. These were called relocation centers; there were ten altogether.

The relocation centers were far from the gentle climate of the West Coast, to which the ethnic Japanese were accustomed. Instead, they were in mountainous areas of Idaho, Wyoming, Arizona, Colorado, Utah, California, and Arkansas. Most of the camps were in bleak deserts where the weather was extremely hot in summer and numbingly cold in winter.

Like the assembly centers, the new relocation centers were surrounded by barbed wire. Sue Embrey remembered the forbidding atmosphere of the camp in which she stayed as a child. "They had eight guard towers. And each one of them had an MP [military policeman] in it with a loaded machine gun. And at night, they had searchlights that followed you wherever you went."

In countless ways, life continued to be starkly different than it was back home. Many of these differences seemed to harm family life. The walls of the barracks did not go all the way up to the ceiling, so people had little privacy. They ate communally, rather than just with family members. The adults had little to do, and their teenage children seemed to drift away emotionally, challenging the authority of their strangely idle parents.

The people in the camps had little contact with the outside world. Caucasian friends and former neighbors could not enter to visit them. Instead, they had to talk through the barbed wire fences. Some friends brought packages, which they had to toss over the fence. Some of the camp dwellers admitted to feeling as if they were in a zoo.

George Takei, the actor who played Lieutenant Sulu on television and in the film versions of *Star Trek*, remembers the childhood years he spent in camps in Arkansas and Northern California. His parents thought up projects that would distract them and help them maintain their dignity, such as creating gardens, celebrating Japanese holidays, and listening to big band music. Takei's teachers were ethnic Japanese. "A . . . teacher taught us how to recite the Pledge of Allegiance to the flag," he said. "I was too young to appreciate the irony of the sight of the barbed wire fence I could see from outside the window."

In 1943, ethnic Japanese who were able to find work and live on their own were allowed to leave the camps and move eastward, to the interior of the country. They could not return home and adults had to pass a loyalty test, which was a type of questionnaire. Once they left the camps, they had to keep the government informed about where they were, like prisoners on parole.

The order banning ethnic Japanese people from the West Coast was lifted in December 1944, about half a year

GEORGE TAKEI, WHO PLAYED LIEUTENANT SULU, THE NAVIGATOR OF THE
Starship Enterprise ON THE TV SERIES *STAR TREK*, IS A JAPANESE
AMERICAN. HE LIVED IN TWO DIFFERENT INTERNMENT CAMPS AS A CHILD.
LIFE IN A CAMP WAS VERY DIFFICULT. TAKEI'S PARENTS TRIED TO THINK
OF ACTIVITIES THAT THE FAMILY COULD ENJOY AND TAKE PRIDE IN, SUCH
AS GARDENING.

before the end of World War II. Gradually the internees were released from the camps. The last center, at Tule Lake, California, closed in March 1946.

The United States Government Apologizes

In the late 1960s and early 1970s, third- and fourth-generation Japanese Americans began demanding some financial compensation for the losses that their families suffered. In response to these demands, the Commission on Wartime Relocation and Internment of Civilians was formed. It conducted hearings across the country for twenty days and heard the testimony of about 750 witnesses, including some of those who had been interned in camps. In its five-hundred-page report, the commission concluded that the internment of ethnic Japanese was not necessary for strategic reasons. It was the result, the commission said, of "race prejudice, war hysteria, and a failure of political leadership."

On August 10, 1988, more than four decades after World War II, President Ronald Reagan signed into law a bill that awarded $20,000 to every American citizen and permanent resident of Japanese ancestry who had suffered significantly during the war. Each check would be accompanied by a presidential letter of apology.

Lessons for a Post–September 11 World

There are some who have studied this sad chapter in American history and concluded that the internment of ethnic Japanese was not a mistake. Among them is Michelle Malkin, the author of *In Defense of Internment: The Case for "Racial Profiling" in World War II and the*

War on Terror. Malkin faults the Commission on Wartime Relocation for not taking into account the evidence of Japan's considerable espionage on the West Coast.

Most historians and legal scholars, however, believe that the U.S. government did, in fact, make a tragic error. Eric Muller, a legal scholar who has written extensively on the internment of ethnic Japanese, described it as "a series of government policies that imposed years of massive physical, spiritual, and economic deprivation on every man, woman, and child of a single national ancestry." The reason for internment, Muller said, was the government's unproven assumption that because of their ancestry, ethnic Japanese were less likely to be loyal to the United States during World War II. Even if some of them viewed Japan as their cultural homeland, he pointed out, there was no reason to assume that they would betray the United States by spying.

Muller believes that the greatest mistake the U.S. government made was in inflicting so much pain on a group of people, "the likes of which," he said, "had not been seen since slavery and the subjugation of Native Americans." No doubt many Japanese Americans would agree. In addition to the great financial losses that they suffered and the years of discomfort that they endured living in camps, they suffered in ways that are more difficult to measure. Some learned to be ashamed of their Japanese heritage.

Satsuki Ina was born in the Tule Lake camp, in California. When her family left the camp, they were advised not to return to California because they would encounter too much prejudice and there weren't enough jobs. Instead, her family moved to an all-white neighborhood in Cincinnati. When Ina entered kindergarten, her teacher gave her an American name—Sandy. "I was called Sandy 'til I was thirty-five," she said. "And it hit me that I had spent most of my life using the wrong name." She changed it back to Satsuki. "It was a very important thing for me to do," she explained, "because my father . . . was a poetry teacher and he gave a lot of thought to that name."

Ina has counseled Japanese Americans who were in camps as children. She has also helped Muslim and Arab American parents whose children were bullied after September 11. The stories she heard were painful reminders of her childhood.

Some scholars and commentators believe that the most valuable lesson we can draw from the internment of ethnic Japanese is that sometimes the government must take away personal liberties for the greater good. During a war, including a war on terror, they argue, our traditional criminal justice system doesn't work. Under extraordinary circumstances, such as World War II and the war on terror, ethnic profiling is necessary.

Most Americans, however, even those who believe ethnic profiling is necessary today, do not see the internment camps as a positive example. They are more likely to agree with those who suffered and declare "Never again!"

2

The Roots of Racial Profiling: From the Mad Bomber to the War on Drugs

Racial profiling, which law enforcement officials have used to catch drug couriers and other criminals, evolved from an older technique of criminal profiling. The older method became popular in the United States in the middle of the twentieth century after a psychiatrist used it with spectacular success to find someone who had been terrorizing New Yorkers.

The Search for the Mad Bomber and the Beginning of Criminal Profiling

In 1940 there was a bomber on the loose in New York. He planted his first bomb at Consolidated Edison, an electric company, but it didn't go off. A year later, he planted another one a few blocks away. Then he was silent for an entire decade while Americans fought overseas in World War II and then recovered from the war.

The bombs were back in New York City in 1950, and this time they were bigger and more destructive. The mystery bomber, who was soon called the Mad Bomber, planted his devices in public places that many New Yorkers visited: libraries, department stores, subways, and theaters, including the famous Radio City Music Hall. He also sent letters to a variety of public figures, including the police, city and state officials, and the head of Con Edison. Decades later, one New Yorker described his childhood fears to a reporter on National Public Radio: "I didn't see any reason why he shouldn't put a [bomb] under my bed!"

By 1956, the Mad Bomber had placed more than thirty bombs around the city. That winter, he detonated one at the Paramount Theater. It was his largest explosion. It injured six people and spread terror throughout the city. The police were under tremendous pressure to find the bomber, but they had run out of clues and were desperate.

Inspector Howard Finney, the director of the New York Police Department's crime laboratory, decided to try a new tactic. He approached James A. Brussel, a local psychiatrist and crime expert.

"We're stumped," the inspector told the psychiatrist. "Here's a bundle of letters and photographs. Solve it."

Brussel was puzzled. "If experts haven't attacked this case, what can a psychiatrist know about it?" he asked.

Inspector Finney smiled. "Give it a whirl, doctor. Sometimes the difference between success and failure is a new thought."

By studying the letters written by the Mad Bomber, as well as photographs of the crime scenes supplied by the police, the psychiatrist began putting together a profile of the sort of person who was planting bombs around New York City. In his letters, the Mad Bomber's old-fashioned phrases and grammar led the psychiatrist to conclude that his family was from central or Eastern Europe. Most im-

GEORGE METESKY, STANDING IN THE CENTER OF THE PHOTOGRAPH, WAS KNOWN AS THE MAD BOMBER. IN THE 1950S, HE PLANTED ABOUT THIRTY BOMBS AROUND NEW YORK CITY. BY EXAMINING A LOT OF EVIDENCE, PSYCHIATRIST JAMES A. BRUSSEL PROVIDED THE POLICE WITH A REMARKABLY ACCURATE DESCRIPTION OF THE MAN WHO WAS TERRORIZING NEW YORKERS.

migrants from that part of the world lived in Westchester County, New York, and nearby southern Connecticut. Brussel guessed the Mad Bomber lived in that region, too. Since the bomber had a sixteen-year-old grudge against the Con Edison company, the psychiatrist concluded that he was a paranoid person. Using a theory of Sigmund Freud, the founder of modern psychiatry, Brussel thought the bomber probably hated his father. He predicted that the man would be living with a sister and, when finally caught by the police, would be wearing a suit, with the jacket buttoned.

Brussel's profile of the Mad Bomber was published in the newspapers on Christmas day: December 25, 1956. A secretary at Con Edison saw the profile and searched the company's files for letters of complaint. She found some written by George Metesky, a former employee who claimed that he was suffering from health problems caused by an accident at a Con Ed power plant. When the police went to Metesky's home, in southern Connecticut, he admitted that he was the Mad Bomber. He was in a bathrobe, but immediately changed to a suit, which he buttoned. Brussel was only slightly wrong about Metesky's housemates. He shared his home with two sisters, not one. The law enforcement world was astonished at the accuracy of Brussel's profile.

By examining evidence, Brussel was able to put together the profile of the sort of person who would behave as the Mad Bomber did. His successful technique inspired others, including Howard Teten, who studied with Brussel. Teten became chief of research at the Federal Bureau of Investigation (FBI), where he helped to further develop the technique of criminal profiling. Teten taught courses on this technique, which spread throughout the FBI.

Criminal profiling was a scientific approach to solving crimes. The purpose of the criminal profile was to identify the *type* of person who was most likely to commit a particular kind of crime, such as murder or arson. One of the FBI's best known profiles was developed to help law enforcement officials find serial killers. It was based on hours of interviews with convicted killers. When a rash of airplane hijackings, or "skyjackings," occurred in the 1960s and early 1970s, a group of experts used similar techniques to help airline workers prevent this type of airline piracy.

Profiling Skyjackers to Make the Skies Safe

On May 1, 1961, a man threatened the pilot of a National Airlines plane with a gun and forced him to fly to Havana, Cuba. The Cuban government did not return him to the United States; he was given permission to remain in Cuba. It was the first time a U.S. aircraft had been hijacked.

There was about one hijacking each year for the next six years. Then in 1968 there were eighteen hijackings, most of them to Cuba. Word had gotten out that Fidel Castro, Cuba's president, would provide a safe haven for Americans who were against their own government or who had committed crimes.

The United States government decided to take action. At first it tried putting specially trained U.S. marshals, called sky marshals, aboard flights that seemed most likely to be hijacked. The marshals didn't help cut down on hijackings, however. The government had to find a way to catch potential hijackers before they boarded airplanes.

Next the government created a task force to attack the problem. This group of experts included people from the Federal Aeronautics Administration, Department of Justice, engineers, psychologists, and lawyers. They recommended some procedures for identifying possible hijackers, including the use of a hijacker's profile. The profile was designed by psychologists and other professionals and was based on a thorough study of previous hijackings. The task force described at least twenty-five characteristics that they thought set potential hijackers apart from other travelers, and then shortened the list for airport personnel. None of these traits were related to a particular racial or ethnic group.

The task force's recommendations were put into effect. Airline workers watched passengers as they came to check in their luggage and collect their boarding passes. If someone seemed to fit the hijacker's profile, his boarding pass was marked without his knowledge. Next, passengers were screened by metal detectors. Anyone who had a boarding pass marked and also set off a metal detector was questioned by airline workers. (If the metal detector uncovered a gun, that passenger would of course be stopped from boarding an airplane even if his boarding pass wasn't marked.)

The procedures recommended by the task force did not reduce the number of hijackings very much, and the hijackings grew more violent. In March 1972, bombs were found on three airliners. In October four hijackers killed a ticket agent. The next month, hijackers forced an airplane to take off after FBI agents shot out its tires. The FAA decided to stop profiling passengers and instead began x-raying all luggage and carry-on bags, which proved to be more effective.

Although the hijacker's profile didn't stop hijacking, it was a stepping stone in the evolution of profiling. In some ways, it was similar to the criminal profiling techniques inspired by James Brussel and developed by Howard Teten and others at the FBI. The hijacker's profile was based on the research and methods of experts in the fields of psychology, for example. But it also differed from criminal profiling in important ways.

Criminal profiling was, and is still, done by trained experts to help law enforcement officials catch people who have already committed crimes. It isn't used to prevent a crime from occurring. The hijacker profile was used to prevent hijackings. Unlike criminal profiling, it wasn't used by experts. It was used by airline workers with little or no training.

The hijacker profile produced an interesting result that its designer had not expected: In late 1972, experts studied the six thousand arrests that were made as a result of the hijacker profile. Less than a fifth of those people were arrested because they had threatened airline safety in some way. But about a third were caught carrying illegal drugs. So when the Drug Enforcement Agency was looking for a way to reduce the quantity of illegal drugs entering the country in the mid–1970s, it came up with a drug courier profile. That profile brought the country closer to the practice of racial profiling.

The War on Drugs

Richard Nixon was the first politician to make illegal drugs a national issue. When he was running for president of the United States on the Republican ticket against Hubert Humphrey in 1968, he needed a focus for his campaign.

Nixon decided to emphasize the need for law and order, or a greater respect for laws and the people who enforce them. In a speech that he gave at Disneyland, in California, before Election Day, he blamed illegal drugs for the turbulence that seemed to be overtaking the United States.

"As I look over the problems in this country," Nixon said, "I see one that stands out particularly. The problem of narcotics." He claimed they were "among the modern curse[s] of the youth," and compared drug use to a plague or epidemic.

Nixon found an issue that many people felt was important. They thought drug use was fueling the youthful rebellion that seemed to be shaking the nation to its rafters. The presidential candidate promised nothing less than a war on drugs, and when he was elected president, he kept his promise.

The government office that was in charge of pursuing drug dealers when Nixon took office did not seem to be very effective. In 1973, the president created the Drug Enforcement Agency (DEA) to conduct his anti-drug war. Inspired by the hijacker profile, the DEA decided to create a drug courier profile.

A Year of Great Turmoil

The year 1968, when Richard Nixon was elected president of the United States, was one of great turmoil and also tragedy for the nation. Americans were divided over the ongoing Vietnam War. Rebellious college students, upset by the war and the possibility that they or their male friends would have to serve in the army, were taking over college buildings instead of going to class.

Many young people, in and out of college, were experimenting with marijuana, LSD, and other hallucinogenic drugs, which temporarily changed a person's perceptions. Some also experimented with alternative lifestyles, such as group living, instead of traditional marriages.

There were other young people, however, who relieved their sense of frustration by becoming involved in the political process. They enthusiastically supported Eugene McCarthy, Democratic senator from Minnesota, who ran in the Democratic primary elections in an attempt to become the Democratic candidate for president. McCarthy strongly opposed the Vietnam War. His young male supporters listened to his campaign's rallying cry, "Come clean for Gene," and cut their long hair and shaved their beards in order to help win him more supporters.

McCarthy was so successful in shaking up the Democractic Party that President Lyndon Johnson, a Democrat, decided not to run for a second term. Another young politician, Senator Robert F. Kennedy, from New York, decided to enter the fray. He was the brother of President John F. Kennedy, who had been assassinated five years earlier.

Tragedy and violence struck several times in 1968: On April 4, Rev. Martin Luther King Jr., a great leader of the civil rights movement, was assassinated, which sparked riots in 125 cities. Two months later, Robert Kennedy was assassinated in California. Then in August, antiwar protesters disrupted the Democratic National Convention in Chicago. Many were beaten in the streets by the Chicago police. At that convention, the Democrats nominated Hubert Humphrey, who was the vice president of the United States at the time.

By then, many middle-aged and older Americans had probably concluded that the nation's long-haired youth were out of control. Richard Nixon provided a scapegoat: The cause of the young people's unrest was illegal drugs, and they had to be eliminated.

AFTER THE GREAT CIVIL RIGHTS LEADER REVEREND MARTIN LUTHER KING JR. WAS ASSASSINATED ON APRIL 4, 1968, PEOPLE RIOTED IN 125 AMERICAN CITIES, INCLUDING WASHINGTON, D.C., WHERE THIS PHOTOGRAPH WAS TAKEN. THE 82ND AIRBOURNE TROOPS ARE SHOWN BREAKING UP THE RIOT.

The DEA's Drug Courier Profile

In 1976, agents from the DEA wanted to stop people from bringing illegal drugs into the country. By then Miami, Florida, had become "the drug capital of the Western Hemisphere," according to the DEA. In 1975 U.S. Custom agents had seized 729 pounds of cocaine, which was almost seven times the amount seized in 1970 (108 pounds).

Special Agent Paul Markonni was the major designer of the DEA's drug courier profile, which was to be used in airports to prevent people from smuggling in drugs on airplanes. He developed the profile after consulting with other agents, drug informants who worked with the government, and even people who were accused of transporting drugs themselves.

The drug courier profile was used by DEA agents in much the same way that airline workers used the hijacker profile. They watched passengers as they boarded and exited from airplanes. If an agent noticed someone who seemed to fit the profile, he identified himself as an agent and questioned the person. Then if the agent was still concerned, he asked permission to search the passenger's luggage and carry-on bags. When the passenger refused, the agent got a search warrant.

Many arrests that were made in connection with the drug courier profile ended up in court. Court records are public documents. So even though the DEA did not reveal the characteristics that made up its drug courier profile, scholars have learned some details through court records. Among the characteristics that DEA agents looked for were people who arrived from or were traveling to a city that was known to have a lot of drug traffic; had very little or no luggage; carried a lot of cash; used a false name; and seemed very anxious.

DEA agents actually seemed to use more than one profile. Some observers noticed that it differed from one region to the next and sometimes from one airport to another. On some occasions, agents apparently considered an airline passenger's race when looking for potential drug couriers. In one court case, for example, a police officer testified that three-quarters of the people who were stopped in the Memphis airport were African American.

The changeable nature of the drug courier profile drew some criticism. One of the critics was Judge George Pratt of the United States Court of Appeals for the Second Circuit, who conducted a survey of court cases that involved the use of the profile. He found many contradictions. Characteristics that were part of one version of the drug courier profile contradicted other characteristics mentioned in another version of the profile. In one version a traveler was suspected because he arrived at his destination late at night. In another, a traveler seemed suspicious because he arrived early in the morning. Someone drew an agent's attention because he acted too nervously, another because he was too calm! Another judge of the same court wondered whether, as a result of the profile, many honest citizens were being questioned. Other courts thought the profile was a useful law enforcement tool.

The DEA's airport drug courier profile was another big step away from the traditional criminal profiling methods practiced by the FBI. It was an even bigger departure than the hijacker's profile. The DEA's profile was not created by skilled psychologists or other scholars, and it was less precise and more changeable. Agents had a lot of freedom when choosing whom to stop at an airport—maybe too much freedom.

The nation's war on drugs was not focused entirely on airports. Those who distributed illegal drugs around the country used the highways, too. Law enforcement officials discovered that using a profile, or profiling, worked on the interstate as well as in airports. It was on the highways, however, that profiling seemed to be a straight road to racial profiling.

Operation Pipeline

When Ronald Reagan became president in 1981, drug smuggling in Florida was rising steeply. A lot of cocaine, in particular, came through Miami. The president was concerned and appointed a group of experts, headed by Vice President George H. W. Bush to focus on South Florida.

With the administration's attention on them, members of the Florida Highway Patrol began looking for drug couriers more aggressively on the state highways. By 1984 they were stopping motorists in large numbers in their search for drug smugglers. Over time, Florida's state troopers developed a drug courier profile for the highway: a list of characteristics they looked for while observing the millions of cars moving along Florida's main roads.

One state trooper, Robert Vogel, has been given more credit than anyone else for developing the profile widely used on the nation's highways. When Vogel stopped drivers for a traffic violation along Interstate 95, he sometimes investigated them for drugs. He noticed that many of the people he caught had some things in common. For example, they often drove large late model or rental cars, drove too cautiously, drove early in the morning, and did not make eye contact with him when he approached them. He began looking for these characteristics, and if he spotted some from a distance, he stopped the driver with the excuse of a traffic violation. His methods were very successful: In one year he arrested thirty people for smuggling drugs. Vogel became a celebrity. DEA agents rode around with him to watch his techniques, and he was interviewed on *60 Minutes,* a highly respected television news program.

Using similar methods, New Jersey troopers were also making a lot of drug seizures along Interstate 95, which ran from Florida all the way to Maine and became known as the drug corridor. In the Southwest, along the highways in New Mexico, state troopers were using profiling techniques to confiscate drugs in record numbers, too. The state troopers referred to their work as "pipeline investigations," which was a reference to the illegal drug pipeline, or distribution network.

As a result of these successes in Florida, New Jersey, and New Mexico, in 1984 the DEA decided to establish a training program to teach state and local law enforcement officers across the country how to profile in order to find drug traffickers on the highways. The program, called Operation Pipeline, eventually reached almost every state in the country.

The highway drug courier profiles varied slightly from region to region, but they shared many of the same characteristics. Law enforcement officers often looked for:

- **Out-of-state license plates (especially New York, Texas, Maryland, and New Jersey) or rental car plates**

- **Guns inside the car**

- **Tools on the floor**

- **Large quantities of cash**

- **Radar detectors**

- **Very little luggage**

- **An ignition key with no other keys attached (such as a house key)**

- **Drug paraphernalia, such as small plastic bags filled with marijuana and scales for weighing it.**

The profiles also noted suspicious behavior, including:

- **Two or more cars driving in a caravan**

- **A driver who looks nervous when a police officer approaches, and cannot look the officer in the eye**

- **A driver who walks toward the police car, as if to avoid having the police approach the driver's car**

- **Unpredictable driving, or the opposite—overly cautious driving.**

Finally, the profiles contained descriptions of the driver. In the 1980s and 1990s, the DEA believed that Colombia, Jamaica, Puerto Rico, Cuba, Mexico, Afghanistan, and other countries in Latin America and Asia were the source of illegal drugs brought into the country. The DEA thought that the drug distribution networks in the United States were often created by gangs of African Americans and ethnic groups whose families came from the countries that were sources for illegal drugs. So it isn't too surprising that racial characteristics were among the traits listed in some profiles to describe suspicious-looking drivers. These traits included:

- **Greasy hair**

- **Shorts worn in winter**

- **Colombian males**

- **Latino males**

- **Young to middle-aged African-American males**

- **Young to middle-aged white males.**

The DEA considered Operation Pipeline extremely successful. Donnie Marshall, a DEA administrator who testified before two subcommittees of the U.S. Senate in 1998, provided some impressive statistics. According to Marshall, during the first nine years of the program, law enforcement officers seized 696,000 kilograms of marijuana, 94,0000 kilograms of cocaine, 642 kilograms of crack, and 278 kilograms of heroin. Critics of highway profiling wondered whether the DEA's program was itself a pipeline—for spreading the practice of racial profiling.

3
Racial Profiling Becomes a National Issue: "Driving While Black"

On April 23, 1998, at about 11 p.m., Keshon Moore was driving a rented silver Dodge Caravan down Interstate 95, heading toward North Carolina. Moore was making the twelve-hour drive with three friends. Danny Reyes sat beside him in the passenger seat, listening to DJ Clue's hip hop tunes, which were blaring from the tape deck. Despite the loud music, Rayshawn Brown and Jarmaine Grant slept soundly in the back seat. All four young men were in their early twenties, and they were all black. They were going to drive all night and arrive in Durham in time to try out for the basketball team at North Carolina State University. The friends had dropped out of their respective colleges, and now they wanted to give college—and their basketball careers—another shot.

A police cruiser pulled up alongside the van and drove next to it for half a mile. Then the cruiser got behind the van, flashing its light to signal Moore to pull over. He was

A PROTESTOR HOLDS UP A SIGN AT AN APRIL 2000 RALLY IN CALIFORNIA AGAINST RACIAL PROFILING. "DWB" STANDS FOR "DRIVING WHILE BLACK." THE EXPRESSION IMPLIES THAT SOMEONE HAS BEEN STOPPED ON THE ROAD BY A LAW ENFORCEMENT OFFICER MAINLY BECAUSE HE OR SHE IS BLACK.

nervous. His license had been suspended because of some unpaid parking tickets.

Two state troopers, white men in their late twenties, got out of the cruiser. One of them approached the van with a gun in one hand and a flashlight in the other. Moore thought he had put the van in "park," but probably because he was so anxious, he had actually put it in "reverse," and the van started rolling back, bumping up against the police cruiser and pushing it backward.

The startled troopers began to shoot. The first bullet cracked the passenger window. Reyes, who was in the passenger seat, shouted "The van's not in park! Stop shooting!" and was trying to grab the gearshift when two bullets pierced his arm. The troopers fired eleven shots altogether, seriously wounding everyone but Moore.

The troopers dragged the young men out of the van and handcuffed them. Then they looked for drugs. Instead of heroin or cocaine, they found bags of potato chips, bottles of Snapple, a Bible, and a copy of John Steinbeck's classic novel, *Grapes of Wrath*. Fifteen minutes later, paramedics finally arrived to examine the young men. None of the friends died, but two were left with permanent injuries.

The troopers were charged with attempted murder and aggravated assault. They were lucky, however, and didn't serve any time in jail. The trial judge decided those charges were too severe and dismissed them. Eventually, he placed the two men on probation.

The incident in New Jersey, covered widely by the media, put the issue of racial profiling on the nation's radar screen. Many assumed the young men were stopped because they were black, and they were outraged. Racial profiling was certainly not news to African Americans and other minorities of color; they were very familiar with this law enforcement practice. That spring night when four young men were shot on the interstate was, for many people, an extreme example of the danger of "driving while black." Others, who supported highway profiling, thought it was a valuable law enforcement tool that two frightened troopers had bungled.

Searching for Drugs on the Highway

The term "racial profiling" wasn't used until the mid–1990s. Long before then, however, state troopers and police looking for drugs went through similar routines, which many had learned through Operation Pipeline. The trooper would park his car at a point along the highway that gave him good visibility for oncoming traffic. If he noticed a suspicious-looking car that in some ways fit the profile his department used to look for drug couriers, he tried to catch the driver committing a moving violation. Since many people drive at least slightly above the speed limit, or forget to use their turn signal, it would be fairly easy for a trooper to catch someone. He did this because if he stopped a person for questioning without a concrete reason for doing so, a judge might later decide that he had violated the person's constitutional rights. The technical term for this strategic stop was a "pretextual stop." The traffic violation provided the trooper with a pretext, or excuse, for stopping the driver.

Once the driver pulled over, the trooper usually asked to see a driver's license and registration. While he waited for the driver to find them, he took the opportunity to look over the vehicle, the driver, and any passengers. He asked the driver where he was going and for what purpose. If the driver said he was going to visit someone, the trooper asked for an address and phone number.

If the trooper suspected that the driver wasn't telling him the truth or that he might, in any case, be transporting drugs, he asked if he could inspect the vehicle. If the driver said no, the trooper advised the driver that he would in that case arrange for dogs to sniff the car. Most drivers consented.

If the trooper found drugs, he arrested the driver. Usually there were no drugs, and he let the driver continue on his way. Occasionally, he gave the driver a ticket. Law enforcement agents assumed that they would have to stop a lot of cars in order to make a drug arrest. One California Highway Patrol sergeant put it this way: " Our guys make a lot of stops. You've got to kiss a lot of frogs before you find a prince. "

Many of those who were pulled over were African American, and in some cases, the same person was stopped many times. For example, an African-American dentist from New Jersey who drove a BMW was forced to pull over one hundred times between 1984 and 1988.

Maryland Troopers
Stop the Wrong Man

In May 1992, Robert Wilkins was driving home to the Washington, D.C., area in the rain after attending his grandfather's funeral in Chicago. With him in a rental car were his aunt, uncle, and a cousin, who was driving. Wilkins and his family were African American.

At the time, some Maryland troopers were looking for blacks using rental cars to transport crack and cocaine. A trooper signaled for Wilkins's cousin to pull over and asked if he could search the car. Wilkins told the trooper that he was a lawyer and did not want the car searched. The trooper requested a dog. While Wilkins's family stood out in the rain, the dog sniffed the car thoroughly and found nothing. Wilkins later commented that he felt helpless. "Part of me feels like there is nothing I could have done to prevent what happened. You know, I was calm and respectful to the police. I tried to explain what my rights are," he said.

Wilkins didn't let the incident pass unnoticed. He had received a law degree from Harvard University and was working in the public defender's office, which provided legal assistance for poor people. He believed the state troopers had violated his rights. So he contacted the American Civil Liberties Union (ACLU), a nonprofit organization that works to protect the rights and liberties of people living in the United States.

The ACLU filed a lawsuit against the Maryland State Police on behalf of Wilkins, his family, and all the other drivers whom the state police had treated in similar ways. The organization accused the police of stopping Wilkins's family and other motorists illegally because of a profile that focused on African Americans in particular. A spokesperson for the state police admitted that African Americans were stopped at a higher rate than whites but argued that this was "an unfortunate byproduct of sound police policies."

The ACLU and the state police reached an agreement: The state police agreed to change their methods of operation and officer training, and avoid targeting African Americans. They also agreed to provide the court with information for the next three years on all of the traffic stops made by the state police. That way, the ACLU could determine whether the state police were keeping their word.

When the ACLU received the data from the court, it gave the information to a statistician by the name of John Lamberth to analyze. Before he analyzed the statistics, Lamberth conducted an unusual survey of his own, which he called a rolling survey. His goal was to determine approximately what percentage of people who were speeding on the highway were African American.

Lamberth had someone drive at the legal speed limit on Interstate 95 north of Baltimore, counting the number of cars that passed him or her on the highway into a tape recorder and noting the race of the driver. According to his survey, about 17.5 percent of the traffic violators were African American. But according to the statistics he received from the Maryland court, 28.8 percent of those who were stopped were African American. In addition, 71.3 percent of those searched were African American. A U.S. District Court judge agreed with Lamberth and the ACLU that Maryland troopers were still using racial profiling.

Racial Profiling Is Under Investigation

In the early 1990s, when Wilkins and the ACLU first brought their suit against the Maryland state troopers, highway profiling was not a hot topic for the media. By the mid–1990s, however, when Operation Pipeline was well-established throughout the country, more African-American drivers were complaining about being pulled over by law enforcement agents. Lawsuits similar to the one in Maryland were filed in Colorado, New Jersey, and Illinois.

Some African-American drivers developed strategies to avoid an encounter with a state trooper. Salim Muwakkil, a Chicago journalist and editor, resisted the temptation of renting a flashy car when he was traveling. Instead of a Mustang, he chose a Taurus in a bland color. He also didn't wear his favorite beret, and he sat up straight, rather than leaning on the armrest. "I know the kind of symbolism I represent when I come through with my tam on, in a gangster lean," he told a *Washington Post* reporter.

Christopher Darden became famous when he was the

prosecutor in the murder trial of the football star O. J. Simpson. Even so, he was stopped about five times a year in his Mercedes, and as he told the *Washington Post*, he always followed a survival strategy: "Once you stop, you just freeze, keep your hand up there on the steering wheel, you don't look around, you don't make any sudden or abrupt movements or gestures." That strategy might have saved the young men in the van on the New Jersey turnpike a lot of emotional and physical pain in 1998.

After that shooting in New Jersey, there was a public uproar. The U.S. Department of Justice investigated the behavior of the New Jersey State Police and concluded that there was a pattern of discrimination against minorities. Many people became aware, for the first time, that some law enforcement agents routinely pulled over minority drivers for pretextual traffic stops in order to search for drugs. The term "racial profiling" suddenly seemed to be on a lot of people's lips. It was commonly used by the media to describe the practice of singling out minorities for minor traffic or criminal offenses in order to look not only for drugs but also for guns and other illegal items.

During this same period, the governor of New Jersey, Christine Todd Whitman, asked the New Jersey attorney general's office to investigate the practices of the New Jersey State Police as well. A task force was appointed, which produced a report in April 1999. The report concluded that New Jersey's state police do, in fact, target minority drivers. Eventually the state of New Jersey entered into a consent decree with the U.S. Department of Justice. According to this legal agreement, the state of New Jersey would stop its law enforcement agents from considering race when deciding whom to stop on the road. In New Jersey, at least, race could no longer be one of the characteristics of a highway drug courier profile.

Crunching Numbers to Uncover Racial Disparities

The New Jersey settlement did not put an end to the public's concern. The respected Gallup polling company, which conducts a variety of surveys, released a poll in December 1999 showing that half of the people polled believed that police around the country practiced racial profiling, and 81 percent disapproved of the practice.

In response to the public's complaints, hundreds of police departments began voluntarily to collect information about traffic stops so that they could analyze their own behavior on roads and highways. In addition, twenty-five states passed laws that made data collection mandatory. Some states focused exclusively on state law enforcement agencies. For example, Kentucky's governor issued an executive order requiring state police to record the race, gender, and ethnic group of everyone they stopped on the road between May and August 2000. The information went to state officials for analysis. Missouri, on the other hand, passed a law in 2000 requiring all police to record the age of the driver stopped, as well as race, gender, ethnic group, the reason for the stop, the type of search the officer conducted, if any, and whether he found illegal drugs or other items, such as guns. Some states are gathering data for a specific period of time, while others are doing it indefinitely.

Collecting data on traffic stops does not eliminate racial profiling. It helps law enforcement agencies see the extent of their problems. It is then up to the state or city to figure out a plan for addressing them. Collecting and analyzing data from police agencies throughout a state are daunting tasks. Massachusetts has been a model of thorough research and analysis.

A Conversation with Jack McDevitt about Racial Profiling

All of the data about traffic stops that police officers have been recording don't actually measure racial profiling, Jack McDevitt pointed out. The director of Northeastern University's Institute on Race and Justice, McDevitt has interpreted information gathered from all over the state of Massachusetts.

"What we've done in our research so far," he explained, "is looked at racial disparities. We as social scientists can't ever measure what caused an officer to stop that person who is in a mall or coming down the street. What we looked at are patterns that may reflect racial profiling."

In addition to the fact that racial profiling is discriminatory, McDevitt thinks it's an inefficient policing tool. He believes that good information, which law enforcement agents refer to as intelligence, is more useful. "The New Jersey State Police switched from profiling as a key means of identifying [drug couriers] to using intelligence-based police work, such as finding out who was selling drugs and where they were going," McDevitt explained. After that switch, they made a spectacular drug arrest. "They pulled over a huge tractor trailer truck that had drugs in it. It didn't fit a typical profile with a fast sports car. You do become more efficient if you use intelligence," he said.

McDevitt added that sometimes there are good reasons for stopping a minority person, which would not be classified as racial profiling. "If you know that two Latinos with Boston Red Sox hats just shoplifted at Abercrombie and Fitch and you see two Latino males with Red Sox hats, then you're going to stop them. That's not racial profiling."

As McDevitt noted, the most common form of profiling isn't based on race—it's based on age. "That might be a good law enforcement strategy," he said, "because young drivers tend to be our worst drivers. And it may be that they need more surveillance. It becomes troublesome if it's not for safety, but because an officer says to himself, 'It's eleven o'clock at night and there are four teenagers in a car, so they must have beer in it, and I'm going to pull them over.' But that being said, black and Latino young people are at higher risk of being profiled [than white kids]."

Massachusetts Takes Action

A team of researchers at Northeastern University's Institute on Race and Justice sorted through the information that local and state police had recorded for the 850,000 traffic tickets they issued between April 2001 and March 2002. The information, which was entered into a database by the Massachusetts Registry of Motor Vehicles, was similar to the information required by Missouri, but details of the search were not asked for or provided.

While they were analyzing the data, the researchers from the institute also met with members of the state's communities and with law enforcement officials to get a more complete picture. They believed that numbers didn't tell the whole story. Jack McDevitt, the director of the institute, and Lisa Bailey, the assistant director of community relations, explained why in an editorial in the *Boston Globe:*

> **Not all disparities are the result of racial profiling; some may be the result of legitimate enforcement practices. If, for example, members of a local neighborhood group from a predominantly African American neighborhood ask the police to enforce traffic laws strictly because they are concerned about speeding cars and the safety of those who live there, the subsequent enforcement actions may disproportionately target African Americans because they are the most common drivers in the neighborhood.**

In January 2004, Northeastern's Institute on Race and Justice released the results of its study of racial profiling in Massachusetts, based on the information recorded by the police and the community-based meetings. They found

RHODE ISLAND ATTORNEY GENERAL SHELDON WHITEHOUSE POINTS
TOWARD AN OVERSIZED MODEL OF A COMPUTER SCAN CARD ON
JANUARY 8, 2001. RHODE ISLAND'S STATE POLICE AND MEMBERS
OF THIRTY-NINE POLICE DEPARTMENTS PLANNED TO USE THOSE CARDS
TO RECORD INFORMATION ABOUT EACH TRAFFIC STOP THEY MADE IN
AN EFFORT TO STOP RACIAL PROFILING.

that 249 police departments, or three-quarters of the
state's 341 departments, showed some racial disparity
when issuing traffic tickets. In Boston, for example, about
a third of the drivers are from minority groups, but they
received half of the traffic tickets.

The state's secretary of public safety ordered 247 departments to collect more information, such as the length
of the traffic stop, the type of road, and the nature of the
search, in addition to the information they had collected
before. This time the state asked police departments to
provide more details on any searches that were conducted.

About two hundred police departments began gathering this data on September 1, 2005, for a one-year period. The police departments may interpret the data themselves after this second round rather than give them to researchers; no definite plans have been made.

Cambridge, Massachusetts, was one of the fifteen communities with the greatest racial disparities for traffic stops. The city's police commissioner, Ronnie Watson, is glad Cambridge police will get a chance to set the record straight. He discovered that officers sometimes checked a box on the traffic citation indicating that they had done a search when, in fact, they hadn't. "They [the state] had us down for 117 searches," he said. "When we audited the citations ourselves, we found there were less than seven searches." Cambridge police cars will soon be equipped with computers and a sophisticated software program to help them create an accurate picture of traffic stops in that city.

Number Crunching Has Its Critics

Not everyone supports the national trend toward gathering information about traffic stops. Some argue that police may stop fewer cars in order to avoid the tedious procedure of recording all the required information. They may also stop fewer African Americans to make the statistics for their department look less biased, save their own jobs, or improve their image in a minority neighborhood.

One criminal justice scholar noted that the more information a police officer was required to record, the more likely he would be to resist doing so. The process often involves handheld computers, for example, which an officer might regard as a nuisance. He thought police departments should instead be encouraged to hire fair, unbiased police officers.

4
The Debate over Racial Profiling

A scene from the late 1990s: An African-American woman who teaches science and social studies to middle-schoolers in New York City is traveling from New York to Baltimore by train. She is visiting her brother and his family in a nearby town. When the train arrives in Baltimore at 1:30 in the afternoon, she is one of the few African Americans getting off.

Outside the station, two undercover African-American policemen approach her. As part of their "cover," they look dirty and unkempt. One of them pulls out a badge. He wants to see her train ticket. Then he asks, "What are you carrying in your bags?"

The schoolteacher goes through a list of items and then asks the two officers, "Why are you stopping me? I just got off the train. I'm out here looking for my brother."

The policemen aren't so sure. They ask her to go inside the terminal. Then they go through her luggage, but they find nothing out of the ordinary.

The experience is humiliating to the schoolteacher, who vows she will never take the train again. From the officers' point of view, they were just doing their job.

A person's reaction to the schoolteacher's experience will be influenced by his or her feelings about racial profiling. A police officer who looks for illegal drugs as part of his or her job might think that although getting pulled over was unpleasant for this teacher, the agents were doing their work as efficiently as possible. It might not make sense to him to require these officers to question Caucasian men in business suits, too. Someone opposed to racial profiling, on the other hand, might say that the teacher's experience is a good example of the unnecessary pain that racial profiling imposes on minorities.

Over time, the definition of racial profiling accepted by many researchers and by the media has broadened. It includes any occasion on which a law enforcement agent uses race as one of several reasons to stop and question a minority person. (Other reasons might be a man's hooded sweatshirt and baggy pants, or the fact that a woman is on a street corner late at night.) The stop can happen in a train station, on the highway, a city sidewalk, or in a mall. Regardless of where a police officer might use this method of fighting crime, it is likely to be controversial.

Some who favor racial profiling as defined in the paragraph above say they are actually against racial profiling. They are using the term in a more narrow sense, to mean questioning someone simply because of his or her race. Many people in the law enforcement community use this narrower definition of the term. In this book, however, racial profiling refers to the broader definition—race is only one trait among several considered by a law enforcement officer.

Arguments in Favor of Racial Profiling

Among the people who offer the clearest arguments in favor of racial profiling are those who work in the law enforcement community, whether they work on streets and highways or teach in a police academy. Others may study criminal justice—the police departments, courts, prisons, and other institutions that enforce the nation's criminal laws (which deal with crimes and punishment). Below are some of the most common explanations they use in support of this law enforcement method.

Minorities Commit More Street Crimes than White People

Those who support racial profiling and researchers who oppose it agree on one fact: African Americans commit a far greater share of the street crimes in the United States than white people. In 1999, for example, surveys of victims of robberies across the nation led researchers to conclude that half of the robberies were committed that year by African Americans. Yet they were only about 12 percent of the population of the United States. (The victims of these robberies were mostly African American as well.)

Many who spend their work day trying to find illegal drug couriers believe that African Americans and Latinos are the foot soldiers of the drug distribution network. According to the El Paso Intelligence Center, which collects national statistics related to law enforcement and illegal drugs, African Americans and Latinos are arrested more often than whites for drug trafficking.

Sociologist Toby Jackson defended racial profiling to catch drug couriers if police do it skillfully. "If drug traffickers are disproportionately black or Hispanic, the police don't have to be racist to stop many minority motorists; they simply have to be efficient targeting potential drug traffickers."

The Arizona Highway Patrol discovered that a particular model and year of pickup truck seen on the interstate highway between Phoenix and Tucson was often stolen.

The driver of a stolen truck was usually of Mexican heritage. Troopers stopped ethnic Mexicans driving this model of truck on the highway between the two cities, but they did not stop white drivers. Some researchers familiar with this example argued that if the troopers had not been allowed to profile, there would have been more stolen trucks on the road.

Many point to these sorts of crime statistics and argue that racial profiling is the most efficient way to pursue some street criminals who deliver drugs, steal trucks, or rob homes. In their opinion, it simply makes good sense. Bernard Parks, the former chief of the Los Angeles Police Department, commented, "In my mind it is not a great revelation that if officers are looking for criminal activity, they're going to look at the kind of people who are listed on crime reports." Parks, who is African American, doesn't believe that police who practice racial profiling, broadly defined, are racist. They are simply doing their job.

When Police Are Forced to Ignore Race, They May Be Less Effective

When Maryland state troopers were repeatedly accused of racial profiling during the 1990s, Mike Lewis, a trooper, became very discouraged. Lewis was unbeatable at sniffing out drugs. He seized one of the largest stashes of crack cocaine in the country. And he was very proud of his instincts. He claimed that he could tell if a man was lying by watching his carotid artery pulse in his neck.

Lewis became frustrated when he suddenly had to worry about whether the African Americans he was pulling over on the interstate would accuse him of racism. He was sure that most of the drug couriers driving on the stretch of highway in Maryland that he patrolled were black. Despite his frustration, the trooper went right on doing his job.

Some people who work in law enforcement or research that field think that when police aren't allowed to profile, they don't do their job as well because their natural instincts lead them to profile. Or they may intentionally arrest fewer African Americans so that they are not branded as racists. Some fear that less aggressive law enforcement will result in more crime. A study conducted in London, in the United Kingdom, in 1999, showed that when police made fewer stops and searches, the crime rate rose.

In Cincinnati, some African Americans rioted for a few days in April 2001 after a police officer shot and killed an unarmed black man. The rioters probably felt, according to one reporter, that the unarmed man had been "racially profiled to death." During the months that followed the riots, the police were afraid of making stops and arrests that would bring more accusations of racial profiling. As a result, they made half as many arrests as usual for nonviolent crimes such as possessing a gun illegally. They also made fewer arrests for violent crimes such as murder and arson (lighting fires), even though there were 20 percent more arsons and murders compared with the same period of time one year earlier.

Police Who Are Forbidden to Use Racial Profiles May Lose Respect for the Law

According to William Stuntz, a professor at Harvard Law School, law enforcement agents believe there is a connection between racial and ethnic groups and some illegal activities, such as drug trafficking. If they are required by the law to ignore that connection, they may lose respect for the law themselves. "If the law asks them to feign ignorance, the likely effect is not to reduce the role ethnicity plays in policing, but rather to reduce the respect the law enjoys among the police. In short, racial and ethnic profiling is a fact of life that the legal system probably cannot change."

Racial Profiling, Broadly Defined, Is a Form of Criminal Profiling

Some defenders choose to call the technique of racial profiling "criminal profiling." They believe that the profiles used by state troopers on highways in Maryland or Arizona are in the tradition of the criminal profiles that the FBI developed decades ago to catch serial killers. Regardless of whether or not a person's race is in a profile, it's a useful, traditional law enforcement technique.

A captain in the New York Police Department uses another term—"target hardening." He views it as a standard police practice that helps police eliminate many people when they are looking for street criminals. "Gender, race, and age are three of the many demographics [traits] police officers use to eliminate people from the mix of who may be stopped for questioning. . . . A thorough knowledge of the area you work in is necessary—who lives and visits there, . . . the physical layout, types of crime occurring. This is part of the target-hardening [or profiling] process that takes place long before an officer sets foot on the gas pedal."

Why People Object to Racial Profiling

Many people have written articles and books criticizing racial profiling. Among them are researchers in the fields of law and criminal justice and members of minority communities. Below are some of their objections.

Racial Profiling Is Less Precise than Traditional Criminal Profiling

Unlike the profiles of serial killers, profiles used to catch drug couriers and other street criminals aren't developed by researchers with special academic training. The profiles used by state troopers and other police looking for illegal drugs or guns are meant to stop a crime while it is happening. Since the law enforcers aren't exactly sure who they are looking for, they pull over a lot of people. The first profiles developed by the FBI, such as the serial killer, were designed to help police find someone who had already committed serial murders.

Racial Profiling Discriminates against Minorities

Equality is one of the most important ideals of the criminal justice system of the United States. The people who write the nation's laws dealing with crimes, the police who enforce these laws, the courts that try people accused of crimes, and the prisons that house those who are convicted are all supposed to work with the ideal of equality in mind. The "Pledge of Allegiance" that so many children recite in school every morning ends with the words "with liberty and justice for all." Many opponents of racial profiling believe, however, that this law enforcement method works against the ideal of equality and discriminates against minorities.

According to one law professor, if people are treated equally, then everyone who commits the same crime should stand an even chance of getting caught, regardless of his or her race, gender, social status, or amount of wealth. Racial profiling works against this ideal by targeting people according to their race, gender, social status, and other traits.

Some African Americans view racial profiling as another chapter in a long history of discrimination. A former police officer, who is African American, was stopped many times when he wasn't in uniform. "We have learned," he said, "there are cars we are not supposed to drive, streets we are not supposed to walk. We may still be stopped and asked, 'Where are you going, boy?'

whether we are in a Mercedes or a Volkswagen."

A young black writer who wrote about the hip hop music industry put it a little differently: "Just because Ice T is rapping about getting paid for selling drugs and putting people who cross him to sleep, why does that mean white people have to follow me around in stores? Or think just because I got loot in my pocket, it's crazy drug money."

Racial Profiling Humiliates People

Some critics of racial profiling admit that it may be an efficient way for police to pursue criminals. But they think it should be abandoned anyway. The humiliation many minority people experience when being searched repeatedly while doing ordinary things like driving on a highway, arriving in an urban train station, or trying to board a bus may leave deep scars.

Sheryl Champen remembers vividly a fall day in 1992 when she was about to board a bus from Oneonta, New York, to New York City, where she was going to visit her sick grandmother. Champen was an admissions counselor at the local state college in town. Not long before her trip to New York City, a burglar had attacked an elderly woman in town. The woman told the police that the burglar was a young African-American male. A police dog followed the scent of the burglar in the direction of the college. So the police interviewed the small population of black male students without any luck. Then they began stopping black men on the streets and questioning them.

When Champen arrived at the bus station in Oneonta, a state trooper asked her for identification, even though she was an African-American woman, not a young male. It was a simple request, but it was humiliating. "When I got on the bus," she told a reporter, "we were all treated, the black people on the bus were treated like we were criminals." People put their bags next to them to discourage

Champen and other African Americans from sitting next to them. When she walked down the aisle to the bathroom, women grabbed their purses, as if she was going to try and rob them. Passengers stared at her and at other African Americans on board the bus.

Champen and a group of African-American men who had been stopped on the street by the Oneonta police filed a lawsuit against the state. The court took up Champen's case separately because she didn't fit the description of the burglar—she was a female. After thirteen years, she won her case. The men are still waiting for theirs to be tried in court.

Racial Profiling Is Bad for Relations Between Minorities and Police

People of color who are frequently questioned by police are likely to become either fearful or resentful. A traffic stop that begins calmly sometimes ends with harsh words. When the person who was stopped knows that his race was one reason he was questioned, he may become hostile, even though the officer has been polite. The officer may then become defensive, and matters can escalate. Occasionally the encounter ends in violence.

Minority people who feel resentful toward police sometimes have useful information that could help the police with an investigation they are conducting. But they may be too mistrustful to share their information. Or minority members of a jury may feel hostile toward the entire legal system.

Randall Kennedy, an African-American law professor at Harvard, noted that the murder trial of the famous African-American football star O. J. Simpson was a wake-up call. "In the aftermath of O. J. Simpson's acquittal, when blacks' accumulated anger at and distrust of the criminal justice system became frighteningly clear," he wrote, "there

A MAN CELEBRATES ON OCTOBER 4, 1995, AFTER THE FOOTBALL STAR O. J. SIMPSON WAS ACQUITTED OF MURDER. ACCORDING TO LEGAL SCHOLAR RANDALL KENNEDY, THE REACTION TO SIMPSON'S ACQUITTAL SHOWED THAT MANY AFRICAN AMERICANS FELT HOSTILE TOWARD THE NATION'S CRIMINAL JUSTICE SYSTEM.

existed widespread recognition of the danger that threatens all Americans when cynicism and rage suffuse [spread through] a substantial sector of the country."

Racial Profiling Strengthens an Association in People's Minds Between Race and Crime

In a letter to the *New York Times,* Ira Glasser, the former head of the American Civil Liberties Union, reminded the newspaper's millions of readers that "even if it is true that most drug dealers are black or Latino [Glasser was skeptical], it does not follow that most blacks and Latinos are drug dealers."

One problem with racial profiling as a law enforcement tool, according to its critics, is that it encourages both the general public and law enforcement officers to think of minorities as criminals, such as drug users, drug traffickers, and burglars. It encourages Caucasian women, for example, to hold on to their pocketbooks or to cross the street when they see young African-American men approaching on a sidewalk.

After Hurricane Katrina rampaged through the Gulf Coast of the United States in 2005, some observant Internet surfers noticed two news photos on Yahoo News, one of a young African-American man and another of a white couple. The photos came from two different news agencies. The African-American man was in water up to his chest. He was holding a case of soda and pulling a plastic bag, which floated on the water. The caption noted that he had been "looting a grocery store." In the photo of the white couple, the woman was holding bags of food. The caption said they were shown "after finding bread and soda from a local grocery store." Anger spread through cyberspace at the strikingly different news descriptions of African American and white people doing the same thing. The African-American rapper Kanye West spoke for a lot of people when he said, "I hate the way they portray us in the media. You see a black family, it says they're looting. You see a white family, it says they're looking for food."

Law enforcement officers may be more likely than civilians to connect race with crime, and racial profiling encourages this association. Bernard E. Harcourt, a law professor at the University of Chicago, believes this is one of its biggest problems. He wrote, "The goal of our law enforcement should not be to aggravate our prejudices about human frailty."

According to some critics, racial profiling makes police officers, as well as civilians, anxious around African Americans and other minorities. As a result, Randall Kennedy points out, racial profiling may actually make police officers less efficient and more likely to make mistakes. It encourages them to lump minorities together, rather than sharply observing the behavior of minorities and Caucasians. "Racial profiling undercuts a good idea that needs more support from both society and the law: that individuals should be judged by public authority on the basis of their own conduct and not on the basis—not even *partly* on the basis—of racial generalization," he wrote.

5
The Courts and Racial Profiling

During the second half of the twentieth century, a handful of court cases determined how law enforcement agents could—and could *not*—use racial profiling. In most of them, the defending lawyers argued that their client's rights, as guaranteed by the Fourth Amendment to the U.S. Constitution, were violated. The first of these court cases was unusual for a couple of reasons. It focused on the actions of the federal government, rather than on law enforcement agents. And the defense based its argument on rights guaranteed by the Fourteenth Amendment, not the Fourth.

Fred Korematsu Challenges the Internment of Japanese Americans

Fred Korematsu was in his early twenties when, on February 19, 1942, President Franklin Roosevelt ordered all

The Fourteenth Amendment to the Constitution

The Fourteenth Amendment was ratified by the states in 1868, after the Civil War. There are five sections. The first was written to protect the rights of African Americans, many of whom were former slaves. Commonly referred to as the "Equal Protection Clause," it has been a legal instrument for fighting discrimination and a cornerstone of civil rights legislation.

The Equal Protection Clause defined the word "citizen" so that it would include former slaves. It prohibited the states from violating the rights of their citizens without proper legal proceedings, or "due process." And it guaranteed that the nation's laws would apply to everyone, and give all "equal protection." The clause reads: "All persons born or naturalized in the United States, and subject to the jurisdiction thereof, are citizens of the United States and of the State wherein they reside. No State shall make or enforce any law which shall abridge the privileges or immunities of citizens of the United States; nor shall any State deprive any person of life, liberty, or property without due process of law; nor deny to any person within its jurisdiction the equal protection of the laws."

FRED KOREMATSU, ON THE LEFT, IS SHOWN ON JANUARY 19, 1983, WITH TWO OTHER JAPANESE AMERICANS, MINORU YASUI, CENTER, AND GORDON HIRABAYASHI. IN THE 1940S, ALL THREE MEN CHALLENGED THE U.S. GOVERNMENT'S RIGHT TO SEND JAPANESE AMERICANS TO INTERNMENT CAMPS. WHEN THIS PHOTOGRAPH WAS TAKEN, THEY WERE DEMANDING THAT THEIR COURT CASES AGAINST THE GOVERNMENT BE REOPENED. A FEW YEARS LATER, THE U.S. GOVERNMENT FORMALLY APOLOGIZED TO KOREMATSU AND ARRANGED FOR REPARATIONS FOR JAPANESE AMERICANS WHO HAD BEEN INTERNED.

ethnic Japanese to leave the West Coast. The United States had just entered World War II, and the government was afraid there might be spies in the Japanese-American community. Korematsu, who was born in California and worked as a welder in the San Francisco shipyards, did not want to leave his Italian-American girlfriend behind. He hoped he would escape the notice of the authorities, but in May he was arrested and eventually sent to an internment camp.

The American Civil Liberties Union (ACLU) of Northern California persuaded Korematsu to file a lawsuit against the U.S. government, claiming the government was discriminating against him. His lawyers argued that his rights, described under the Equal Protection Clause of the Fourteenth Amendment, had been violated by Roosevelt's order. Korematsu's case, *Korematsu v. United States*, eventually reached the Supreme Court in 1944. The Court ruled that the government had the right to keep Korematsu out of a large portion of the West Coast, which the government had declared a military zone. It denied this was an act of racial bias.

Forty years after Korematsu was convicted, a team of lawyers reopened his case, which was tried in a district court. The court overturned Korematsu's criminal conviction. In a strongly worded opinion, the judge wrote about the decision: "Korematu remains on the pages of our legal and political history. . . . [I]t stands as a constant caution that in times of international hostility and antagonisms our institutions . . . must be prepared to protect all citizens from the petty fears and prejudices that are so easily aroused."

Fred Korematsu became an active defender of civil rights. In 2004, he wrote an editorial in the *San Francisco Chronicle* in defense of the rights of Arab and South Asian Americans after the attacks of September 11, 2001. "Fears and prejudices directed against minority communities are too easy to evoke and exaggerate. . . . I know what it is like to be at the other end of such scapegoating and how difficult it is to clear one's name after unjustified suspicions are endorsed as fact by a government."

The Courts Take a Fresh Look at the Fourth Amendment

In modern times, the Supreme Court allowed two types of encounters between police and citizens as a result of the Court's interpretation of the Fourth Amendment. In a voluntary encounter, a police officer could approach someone and ask him or her a variety of questions. If the person preferred not to answer, that was fine. In what became known as an "involuntary stop," a police officer could question someone against his or her will if there was "probable cause," or a likelihood that a crime had occurred. The Court applied similar rules to searches. They could be done without a warrant if the police officer had the permission of the person who was being searched and there was "probable cause" for doing so. If the person refused to be searched, the police officer needed a warrant. When a search was done without probable cause, it was an illegal search. A court could exclude as evidence anything that a police officer found through an illegal search, such as guns or drugs.

In the case of *Terry* v. *Ohio*, which the Court decided in 1968, the Court interpreted Fourth Amendment differently. This new interpretation affected the future of criminal profiling and helped to make racial profiling a reality.

A Supreme Court Case Hands Police Officers More Power

Terry v. *Ohio* was about an involuntary stop without "probable cause" or the probability that a crime had occurred. Martin McFadden, a plainclothes police detective, spotted two men outside of a store in the city of Cleveland, Ohio. McFadden thought the two men, John Terry and Richard Chilton, were behaving suspiciously and might be

The Fourth Amendment

Five important court cases connected with racial profiling were argued toward the end of the twentieth century. Four came before the Supreme Court. All five hinged on the courts' interpretation of the Fourth Amendment.

The Fourth Amendment is among the ten amendments to the U.S. Constitution that form the Bill of Rights. These amendments were written to provide additional protection for the basic rights of American citizens, such as freedom of speech and religion. They were ratified by the states in 1791, just three years after the U.S. Constitution was ratified. In fact, Virginia, the last state to approve the Constitution, would only do so after promises were made to add a bill of rights.

The Fourth Amendment is about searches and seizures. Before the colonists won the War of Independence, British officials could legally enter anyone's home and search and take their belongings without demonstrating a good reason to do so. They did not require a warrant, which is a legal document. The Fourth Amendment made this sort of behavior illegal. It reads: "The Right of the people to be secure in their persons, houses, papers, and effects, against unreasonable searches and seizures, shall not be violated, and no Warrants shall issue, but upon probable cause, supported by Oath or affirmation, and particularly describing the place to be searched, and the persons or things to be seized."

casing the store in order to rob it. When McFadden approached the two men and asked their names, they muttered. After a brief conversation, McFadden patted them down to see whether they were carrying guns. McFadden's reason for patting them down was based on some sharp observations, rather than "probable cause." McFadden was right. He did find guns on them, and he charged them with carrying concealed weapons.

During their court hearing, Terry and Chilton's lawyers argued that their guns should not be considered as evidence against them because the pat-down was "unreasonable" and McFadden had neither "probable cause" nor a search warrant. The lower courts decided against Terry and Chilton. By the time the case reached the Supreme Court, Chilton had died.

The Supreme Court decided that when McFadden stopped and patted down Terry, he did not violate the Fourth Amendment. The Court ruled that this search was reasonable, even though McFadden didn't have "probable cause." In the Court's opinion, McFadden had a reasonable suspicion that the two men were about to commit a crime, and that was acceptable. As a result of this decision, from 1968 to the present, a police officer can make similar involuntary stops and pat-downs if he or she has reasonable suspicion. *Terry v. Ohio* made it legal for law enforcement agents to stop and search people on the basis of a profile, including the drug courier profile.

The Supreme Court Examines the Behavior of Border Patrols

The Supreme Court has touched on the issue of racial or ethnic profiling in only a few cases. One decision, the *United States v. Martinez-Fuerte*, was not about a profile, but it dealt with the issue of questioning someone mostly

U.S. Border Patrol agents are standing watch over a group of illegal immigrants, who are probably Mexican, in May 2001. In the case *United States v. Martinez-Fuerte*, the Supreme Court concluded that under some circumstances, border patrol officers could stop people for questioning mainly because of their racial or ethnic background.

because of his or her ethnic identity. At a U.S. Border Patrol checkpoint between Mexico and the United States, a patrol officer who was probably looking for illegal immigrants questioned some people in a vehicle who looked Latino. In its 1976 decision, the Court argued that it was reasonable for the officer to investigate the people in the vehicle, even though he did so mostly because they appeared to have Mexican ancestors. The Court noted that the "intrusion [in the stop] is sufficiently minimal that no particularized reason need exist to justify it."

The Supreme Court Considers the Drug Courier Profile

In 1989 the Court ruled on whether agents of the U.S. Drug Enforcement Agency (DEA) could legally stop and search someone because he or she showed some of the characteristics of a drug courier profile.

Andrew Sokolow and a companion had just returned to Honolulu National Airport from a trip to Miami. The agents noticed them and became suspicious of Sokolow for a number of reasons: he paid for both plane tickets in cash; brought only one carry-on bag; and had only been in Miami (a known source for illegal drugs) for twenty-four hours, even though the round-trip took twenty hours. In addition, Sokolow was traveling under his mother's maiden name, and not his own.

When the DEA agents asked Sokolow's permission to inspect his luggage, he refused. The agents brought drug-sniffing dogs, which seemed to be alerting the agents that there were indeed drugs. The agents got a warrant next and inspected the luggage, which contained 1,063 grams of cocaine.

When the *United States* v. *Sokolow* reached the Supreme Court, the Court was interested in the question of whether the DEA agent who had observed Sokolow had a reasonable suspicion before stopping him, as the Fourth Amendment demanded. The Court decided that the DEA agent acted properly. The fact that his suspicions were based on a profile did not bother the majority of the Court. It noted in its opinion that "[T]he fact that these factors may be set forth in a 'profile' does not somehow detract from their . . . significance as seen by a trained agent."

The nine members of the Supreme Court vote on each case that they consider, and the majority decides the case. The Court's written opinion expresses the views of the majority. But sometimes, the members of the Court who disagree with the decision write their own dissenting opinion. Justice Thurgood Marshall disagreed strongly with the Court's decision in the *United States v. Sokolow*. In his dissenting opinion he objected to the use of the profile. He noted that many innocent people make short trips to resort cities like Miami, and they may take only one carry-on bag. Paying for tickets in cash, he pointed out, didn't indicate that someone was going to commit a crime. He disagreed with the majority's claim that the agent's use of a profile was not important. "On the contrary, the majority thus ducks serious issues relating to a questionable law enforcement practice," Marshall wrote. It was the last time the Supreme Court focused directly on profiling as a law enforcement technique.

The Supreme Court Looks at a Traffic Stop

In 1996 the Supreme Court considered a case about a traffic stop. Although the details of the case may not seem out of the ordinary, the Court's decision had enormous consequences.

In a place that was known to be a source of illegal drugs, two police officers were on duty in an unmarked police car. They noticed two young African-American men in a car with temporary license plates. The police thought the car paused at a stop sign for an unusually long period of time. After the driver turned without signaling and took off, the police followed and pulled him over. When they approached the vehicle, they saw that the passenger, whose last name was Whren, had a bag of cocaine in each of his hands. The police arrested him on drug charges.

Whren's defense lawyers argued that the traffic stop was a violation of the Fourth Amendment because the police did not have any reasonable suspicion that Whren had drugs. The lawyers asked the court to ignore the evidence—the cocaine—because the search was illegal. They also argued that the police stopped the two men in the first place because of their race.

The government claimed that the driver's traffic violations gave the police the necessary "probable cause" to stop Whren's car. (The violations included failing to signal before making a turn and driving too fast.) The government admitted that the police officers may have intended to investigate Whren's car for drugs in the first place, and they didn't have probable cause to do so. But the government argued that the true interest of the police didn't matter, and once they saw the cocaine they could legally make an arrest.

When the Supreme Court voted on *Whren* v. *United States*, the decision was unanimous. The Court ruled in favor of the government. It decided that when a police officer notices a traffic violation, he or she has "probable cause" to stop the car, no matter what the officer's real interests are. He can stop someone for a traffic violation as a pretext, or excuse, with the hope of finding drugs or guns.

The Court briefly turned its attention to the question of whether the officers stopped the men because of their race. It argued that it could not guess at the motives of the officers. If Whren's lawyers wanted to argue that the police discriminated against him, they would have to file a separate lawsuit and base their case on the Equal Protection Clause of the Fourteenth Amendment.

Some legal scholars believe that the Supreme Court refused an opportunity to comment on some very important issues. By the time the Court ruled on Whren, enforcement officers around the country were using traffic stops to find drug couriers. Robert Wilkins, who felt he was the victim of racial profiling, had already brought a lawsuit against the state police of Maryland. A New Jersey state trial court had just handed down a decision on racial profiling in

New Jersey v. *Pedro Soto*. A national debate on the twin issues of racial profiling and pretextual traffic stops was brewing.

Whren v. *United States* was a gift to the law enforcement community because it increased an officer's opportunity to stop and question someone in a vehicle. All the driver had to do was commit a traffic violation. As the legal scholar David Harris pointed out, there are so many traffic rules that it may be hard *not* to commit a violation when driving. While these rules may be part of a state's or city's traffic code, many are simply not enforced. "Police officers in some jurisdictions have a rule of thumb," he wrote. "The average driver cannot go three blocks without violating some traffic regulation."

A New Jersey Judge Examines Evidence of Racial Profiling

In 1990, a group of criminal lawyers in New Jersey challenged the state troopers' methods of stopping vehicles on the highway to search for drugs. The case was similar to *Whren* v. *United States*. The defendants were African-American clients of these lawyers who believed they had been targeted on the highway because of their race. The state troopers had found drugs or other illegal items in the defendants' vehicles. Their lawyers argued that the state troopers had obtained these items through illegal traffic stops. The troopers had decided to stop their clients, the lawyers argued, because of their race. The lawyers asked the court to therefore suppress, or exclude, this illegally gotten evidence from each defendant's criminal case.

The group case, *State* v. *Pedro Soto*, reached the New Jersey Superior Court in November 1994. Judge Robert Francis agreed to look at a lot of statistics about traffic stops in New Jersey. He was most impressed by the data gathered by John Lamberth, who conducted a rolling survey similar to the one he later did in Maryland for the defense of Robert Wilkins. Lamberth showed that of the 42,000 cars he observed on Interstate 95 in New Jersey, African-American and white drivers violated the speed limit at the same rate. About 13 percent of these cars had a black driver or passenger. Of those arrested on the highway, 73 percent were African American.

In 1996, after considering all of the evidence, Francis decided that New Jersey state troopers had been targeting African Americans on the interstate for a long time. He concluded that was the only logical explanation of the gap between the small percentage of African-American drivers on the road and the large percentage of African Americans among those who were stopped and arrested on the interstate. As a result, he granted the defense attorneys' request to exclude anything the troopers found in the defendants' vehicles as evidence.

Judge Francis's decision made the legal community and the public more aware of the issue of racial profiling. It did not, however, influence the Supreme Court's decision in *Whren v. United States*. Some court watchers were surprised that a state court proved to be more sensitive to the issue of race than the Supreme Court. Two scholars, Milton Heumann and Lance Cassak, pointed out that earlier in the twentieth century the Supreme Court had been a greater champion of civil rights than the state courts.

6
Did September 11 Change Everything?

In December 1999, Americans were excited about witnessing the arrival of the year 2000, as were people around the world. But they were also anxious. The State Department had received reports that terrorists would attack American citizens during the millennium festivities, and the department was advising Americans to avoid large celebrations. Everyone remembered the day the World Trade Center in New York City was bombed in 1993. Six people died as a result and more than one thousand were wounded. So as the year 2000 got closer, law enforcement officials in the United States were watchful.

On December 14, a slim, dark-haired man in his late twenties was stopped for routine questions by a border patrol in Washington State. The man had just driven off the ferry from Vancouver, in western Canada. The inspector asked him a few questions and noticed that he seemed very nervous. So he asked the man to get out of his car. At first the man refused. Then he got out of his car and ran, forcing customs officials to chase him on foot through the town. He was finally arrested six blocks from the ferry terminal.

THIS EVIDENCE EXHIBIT SHOWS PART OF AN EXPLOSIVE DEVICE, ACCORDING TO THE PROSECUTORS WHO HELPED CONVICT AHMED RESSAM OF TERRORISM. RESSAM PLANNED TO SET OFF BOMBS AT THE LOS ANGELES INTERNATIONAL AIRPORT DURING THE MILLENNIUM CELEBRATIONS.

The customs officials were astonished at what they found in the car: 150 pounds of chemical explosives and four bomb detonators. The chemicals were the same type that were used in the 1993 bombing of the World Trade Center. There were also maps of Washington and California in the car. Although the name on the man's fake passport was Benni Noris, his real name was Ahmed Ressam. He was an Algerian who had once trained in Afghanistan with Al Qaeda, Osama bin Laden's terrorist organization. Ressam was planning to detonate bombs at the busy Los Angeles International Airport around New Year's.

The customs official who first stopped Ressam probably saved many lives. Did he stop Ressam because he looked like he came from a Muslim nation, in addition to the fact that he seemed so anxious? In that case, he was using ethnic profiling.

September 11 Rekindled the Racial Profiling Debate

Less than a year after Ressam's arrest, on September 11, 2001, the World Trade Center was attacked again, along with the Pentagon in Washington, D.C. This time, almost three thousand people died, including the passengers and crew of a hijacked airplane that crashed in Pennsylvania. It was one of the single worst acts of terrorism in the world's history.

In the United States, life did not seem the same after the attacks. A national tragedy left Americans feeling sad, angry, and also fearful. On television news reports and in the newspapers, political experts and ordinary people commented again and again, "September 11 changed everything."

Americans certainly did not feel as secure as they had before the attacks. Most people wanted reassurance from the government that it was doing all it could to prevent another one. Many thought that in airports, subways, and other potential terrorist targets, law enforcement officials should keep an eye on young men who looked Arab, like the 9/11 terrorists and like Ahmed Ressam.

Others disagreed. A month after the attacks, a group of experienced intelligence specialists sent a memo to American law enforcement officials around the world.

They warned the officials not to use ethnic and racial profiling because it wasn't effective. Instead, they urged them to focus on people's behavior.

Once again, racial and ethnic profiling was hotly debated. But the risk of being on the wrong side of the debate seemed much greater. Terrorists who slipped across the border into the United States or drove down an interstate highway, unnoticed, were much more dangerous than drug traffickers.

The possibly horrific consequences of having terrorists in their midst seemed to change people's opinions. Before 9/11, polls showed that 60 percent of the U.S. population believed racial and ethnic profiling was unfair and a poor law enforcement method. After the day that "changed everything," 60 percent of those who were polled said they were in favor of profiling people with Middle Eastern and foreign Muslim backgrounds.

Civilians Do Their Own Profiling

In the first couple of months after the attacks, some American citizens were doing their own profiling. They directed their anger at Arab Americans and people who looked as if they might be Muslim, such as those whose families came from South Asia. There were hundreds of violent incidents. Some people became very nervous when they boarded an airplane along with men who looked Middle Eastern or South Asian. Sometimes, they even demanded that these men be taken off the plane.

On New Year's Eve, 2001, Edgardo Cureg, who was a graduate student in mathematics at South Florida, was returning to Florida from London. Cureg, who was thirty-four years old, was originally from the Philippines. When he changed planes in New Jersey, he met up with one of his professors, who was from Sri Lanka, and a friend born in

Guyana who was a U.S. citizen. All three men were going to Tampa, Florida.

After the men settled into their neighboring seats on the airplane, they noticed that a woman passenger was glaring at them. The passenger summoned the captain and said, "Those brown-skinned men are behaving suspiciously." The captain did not talk with the men; he simply had them removed.

Many Americans would have found the behavior of the woman on the airplane shocking. Some made a point of reaching out to Arab Americans and Middle Easterners. The country's political leaders helped, too. Hussein Ibish, of the American-Arab Anti-Discrimination Committee, told a radio talk show host, "I think the intervention of people like the President . . . people in Congress, [and] lots of prominent Americans across the board calling for tolerance helped a great deal."

Muslims and Arab Americans still receive suspicious glances, though. Some sense the watchful eyes of the government as well.

The U.S Government Weighs Civil Liberties Against Security

Soon after the terrorist attacks, Supreme Court Justice Sandra Day O'Connor paid a visit to New York. She went to Ground Zero, where the twin towers of the World Trade Center once stood, and then spoke at New York University Law School. "We're likely to experience more restrictions on our personal freedom than has ever been the case in our country," she warned.

During the first few years after September 11, which was immediately nicknamed "9/11," the U.S. government took a variety of steps to protect the country against more terrorist attacks. Some of these measures gave the government more power to monitor people, in the hopes of

THE OMAR MOSQUE IN PATERSON, NEW JERSEY, SHOWED ITS
OPPOSITION TO TERRORISM JUST DAYS AFTER THE 9/11 TERRORIST
ATTACKS. IBRAHIM SALEM, LEFT, AND HIS BROTHER RAED, MIDDLE,
PUT UP THE SIGN.

catching any terrorists in the country. At the same time, they put some limitations on people's civil liberties, the basic freedoms that are protected by the Bill of Rights, just as Justice O'Connor predicted. Many people hardly noticed these changes. Others found them impossible to ignore, including Arab Americans and Muslims whose families came from northern Africa, South Asia, and the Middle East.

Congress Approves the USA Patriot Act

In October 2001, long before Americans knew exactly how many died on September 11, Congress quickly passed a 342-page bill to help fight terrorism. The USA Patriot Act gave the government sweeping powers to gather information on American citizens and foreigners staying in the country. A lot of people worried about losing precious civil liberties. One research organization reproduced the Fourth Amendment on its Web site with the dates 1789–2001, as if the amendment had just died. The people who probably were most concerned about the new act were Arab Americans and Muslims.

Among the sections of the act that bothered the American-Arab Anti-Discrimination Committee was Section 215. That section allows the government to gather a variety of records—from the books a person checks out of a library to medical records and records from a mosque, church, or synagogue. In the past the government could only request these records if it had "probable cause" that a crime had taken place or might soon, as required by the Fourth Amendment. Now, the government could demand these records from the library or a doctor's office by claiming it was fighting terrorism. Mary Rose Oakar, the president of the American-Arab Anti-Discrimination Committee, said she was afraid that Section 215 would make it

Librarians Oppose Sections of the USA Patriot Act

About 64,000 librarians belong to the ALA. Librarians often feel passionately about the role of a library in a community. It's a place where people can go to search freely for all sorts of information they may need. The ALA is against any provision of the Patriot Act that makes library patrons feel as if the government may be looking over their shoulders, monitoring the books they take out of the library and the Web sites they view from the library's computers. In its formal resolution on the Patriot Act, the ALA proclaimed,

> **Whereas the American Library Association holds that the suppression of ideas undermines a democratic society; and/ Whereas privacy is essential to the exercise of free speech, free thought, and free association; and, in a library, the subject of users' interests should not be examined or scrutinized by others. . . . Resolved that the American Library Association opposes any use of governmental power to suppress the free and open exchange of knowledge and information.**

In the same resolution, the ALA urged Congress to hold hearings in order to learn the extent to which the government has been examining the reading habits of some library patrons. It also urged Congress to become active in overseeing the ways in which the Patriot Act is used by the government.

legal for the government to target Arab Americans and Muslims.

The other sections that especially troubled the ADC were sections 411 and 412, which are directed at foreigners who are staying in this country. If they associate with an organization that the government believes is a terrorist group, the United States can send them back to their native countries. In addition, the attorney general can keep a foreigner in a prison or another secure place indefinitely if he believes that person is a threat to the country.

The ADC wasn't the only organization that opposed sections of the Patriot Act. Organizations concerned about the loss of civil liberties, such as the American Civil Liberties Union, weren't happy with it either. One of the most vocal organizations was the American Library Association (ALA).

The Justice Department Interviews Thousands of Middle Eastern Men

In November 2001, about a month after the Patriot Act was approved, the attorney general, John Ashcroft, made a startling request. He asked police chiefs around the country to help the Justice Department and the Federal Bureau of Investigation interview about 5,000 young Middle Eastern men. The purpose of the interviews was to help gather intelligence, or information, on terrorist enemies. Ashcroft assured the police that the interviews would be voluntary, and the men would not have to cooperate.

The attorney general's request made some of the police chiefs very uncomfortable. The plan seemed like racial profiling to them, and they were concerned about upsetting the Arab-American communities in their cities. Detroit's chief of police, Charles Wilson, was given a list of 83 names. He said his officers didn't want to "go out and treat people like criminals." A reporter for the *New York Times* noted that the Justice Department and the police chiefs seemed to have reversed roles. Not too long ago the

AFTER 9/11, THE BUSH ADMINISTRATION HAD NO TROUBLE PASSING THE USA PATRIOT ACT, BUT MANY PROTESTED ATTORNEY GENERAL JOHN ASHCROFT'S PLANS TO INTERVIEW MEN OF MIDDLE EASTERN BACKGROUND. ARTIST ERIC BROWN OF NEWARK, NEW JERSEY, DISPLAYS A PAINTING DEPICTING THE FRUSTRATION, ANGER, DESPAIR, AND FEAR PEOPLE FEEL IN THE FACE OF RACIAL PROFILING.

Justice Department had been cautioning them against racial profiling on the highways.

When, the following March, the attorney general announced that he wanted to interview 3,000 more foreigners, the American-Arab Anti-Discrimination Committee lost its patience. They, too, accused the Justice Department of racial profiling.

President Bush Bans Racial Profiling—Most of the Time

When George W. Bush ran for president in 2000, he promised to do something about racial profiling. Early in his presidency, he declared, "It is wrong, and we will end it in

America." He was referring mainly to law enforcement agents who were profiling African Americans and Latinos. After 9/11, his administration received many complaints that the government was profiling Middle Eastern men in an effort to fight terrorism.

In June 2003, President Bush announced new guidelines on racial profiling that forbid federal law enforcement officials from using this technique in most, but not all, situations. The guidelines applied to seventy federal agencies. A federal agent looking for drug traffickers, for example, could not concentrate on a particular neighborhood simply because most residents were African American.

The new guidelines allow ethnic and racial profiling, however, for some terrorist investigations. If the government was informed that some terrorists from Bali were going to blow up a train station in Chicago, the government could order law enforcement officials to pay special attention to people who looked South Asian in Chicago's train stations.

The American Civil Liberties Union (ACLU) criticized the new guidelines. Laura Murphy, the director of the ACLU's Washington, D.C., office, pointed out that no provisions had been made to enforce them. And they did not apply to state or local law enforcement agencies. Ibrahim Hooper of the Council on American-Islamic Relations commented, "There seem to be a lot of 'buts' and 'howevers' here that would allow profiling of Arabs and Muslims to continue."

Bombings in London Hit Home

On July 7, 2005, four suicide bombers attacked three subway trains in London and a double decker bus, killing fifty-six people. The attacks were carried out by young men who were born in Britain, a fact that shocked and chilled the nation. Two of the men had Pakistani ancestors and one had Jamaican ancestors. A couple of weeks after that bombing, another four men attacked similar targets in London, but the bombs failed to detonate.

Then on July 22, another tragedy made the news in that jittery country. Police in plainclothes were watching a well-kept housing project in London. They had found the address in the backpack of one of the failed bombers. The police didn't realize there was more than one apartment in the building. They assumed that whoever walked out of it was coming from the address in the bomber's backpack.

When Jean Charles de Menezes, an electrician, left the building to go to work, the police followed him. They trailed his bus and surrounded him when he entered a subway station. The police asked him to stop. He was wearing

JAI SINGH, WHO IS EIGHTEEN, STANDS ON WHITECHAPEL ROAD, IN LONDON, AND READS A NEWSPAPER ARTICLE ABOUT A SUICIDE BOMBER ON JULY 27, 2005. EARLIER THAT MONTH FIFTY-SEVEN PEOPLE WERE KILLED BY BOMBS SET OFF ON THREE SUBWAY TRAINS AND A BUS.

a bulky jacket despite the warm weather, and the police were afraid he was carrying a bomb.

De Menezes ran down the escalator and tried to get on a train, but the police shot and killed him. They soon learned that de Menezes, who was born in Brazil, was no terrorist. He ran because he was scared.

The bombings and the shooting of de Menezes, which traumatized Britain, produced aftershocks in the United States. The bombings seemed very close to home. If they could happen on a London subway, couldn't they also happen in New York, Boston, or San Francisco? For weeks it seemed impossible to read a newspaper or listen to a news show on the radio or television without hearing a discussion about how to make the United States more secure. Despite Jean de Menezes's terrible death, one controversial solution that seemed to come up again and again was racial and ethnic profiling.

The Arguments for Ethnic Profiling after 9/11

After the London bombings, New York's mayor, Michael Bloomberg, asked the city's police to take extra precautions to protect the subways. He wanted them to search subway riders' bags, such as briefcases, backpacks, and large pocketbooks. They couldn't examine everyone's bags, of course. So Bloomberg decided that the inspections would be completely random. There would be no profiling.

Some people shook their heads over the mayor's decision. One researcher, Paul Sperry, spoke for a lot of people when he wrote, "Young Muslim men bombed the London tube [subway], and young Muslim men attacked New York with planes in 2001. . . . Unfortunately, however, this demographic group won't be profiled. Instead, the authorities will be stopping Girl Scouts and grannies in a procedure that has more to do with demonstrating tolerance than with protecting citizens from terrorism." Sperry had summed up one of the most common arguments for ethnic profiling.

Focusing on People Who Most Resemble Terrorists Makes Sense

Grandmothers, Girl Scouts, and young children come up from time to time in the national conversation about racial and ethnic profiling. To some, they symbolize the ridiculousness of random searches in subway stations and airports. Who could imagine a sweet-faced, gray-haired woman getting on the subway at Times Square, in New York City, with a bomber's belt under her coat?

The faces of the terrorists that appeared in the newspapers after 9/11 all looked Middle Eastern. How, one political commentator wondered after the attacks, could law enforcement *not* focus on Middle Eastern men? "We're at war with a terror network that just killed [thousands] of innocents and has anonymous agents in our country planning more slaughter," he said. "Are we really supposed to ignore the one identifiable fact that we know about them?"

Another writer argued that airport screeners could make flying in a commercial plane instantly safer by using well-designed profiles that take a person's ethnic background into account. People who looked Middle Eastern but had obviously lived in the United States for a long time should not be singled out, he noted. He thought that if airport screeners and law enforcement officers had used such a profile, they would have noticed the September 11 hijackers, who brought box cutters onto commercial jets.

A few Arab Americans agreed that airport screeners should pay attention to what they can see most easily—a person's face. Fedwa Malti-Douglas, a university professor, flies often, and she is used to being taken aside.

"My American passport says I was born in Lebanon," she wrote in a newspaper editorial. "I have an unusual name and a classic Mediterranean appearance. . . . Once while flying on El Al [airline] from Cairo to Tel Aviv, my husband and I were seated in the front and the crew watched our every move." Another time, in Zurich, Switzerland, Malti-Douglas was taken to a bare airplane hangar, where her suitcases were unpacked. Someone suspected she might have a bomb in her suitcase. "Despite the inconvenience to me," she explained, "I believe this scrutiny is a defensible tactic for picking out potential problem passengers. Although I am not a terrorist, others do not necessarily know it. The airline security procedures I ran into also protect me from terrorism."

Ethnic Profiling Saves Precious Time and Resources

Those who support ethnic profiling to fight terrorism often note that it's an efficient shortcut. Peter Schuck, a professor at Yale University, explains it this way: A security officer in a railroad station who is looking out for possible terrorists must scan crowds of people as they quickly pass through his or her line of vision. If he stops many people to question them, he may create impossibly long lines. But he doesn't want to miss the one person who might in fact be a terrorist. Schuck notes that a person's physical traits, gender, and dress are important clues. "No one would think it is unjust," Schuck explained, "for our officer to screen for Osama bin Laden, who is a very tall man with a beard and turban, by stopping all men meeting that general description."

Schuck pointed out that people often do something similar to profiling without even thinking about it. They draw some conclusions about strangers by their physical appearance and behavior. If a large man with an angry expression on his face is walking down the street, the most natural reaction would be to avoid him.

Profiling Is the Best Choice Because the Stakes Are So High

No one likes to think about what might happen if an airport screener or a police officer missed someone with a bomb inside a coat or backpack. Some people argue that even though ethnic profiling creates difficulties for innocent people, it is a fair practice. They believe that profiling offers one of the most accurate ways to identify potential terrorists and avoid another great tragedy. From their point of view, this enormous advantage makes the cost of profiling the innocent people who are stopped repeatedly because they look Arab or Muslim seem insignificant.

A columnist for the *New York Times* summed up the argument: "El Al, the Israeli airline, has the world's most effective security system, and it's all about racial profiling. . . . As risks change, we who care about civil liberties need to realign balances between security and freedom."

Arguments Against Profiling, Even in a World with Terrorism

In 2002, Jose Padilla was arrested in Chicago as an enemy combatant. He was accused of helping four other men raise money for terrorist activities in Afghanistan and other parts of the world. Intelligence officers learned of Padilla's activities because they were able to wiretap his phone as a result of their expanded powers under the Patriot Act. Padilla and his accomplices talked in code, sometimes mentioning vegetables. They discussed zucchini, for example, and "green goods," which the government thought might be weapons.

Padilla, thirty five years old, is an American who once belonged to a Chicago gang. He might easily slip past an airport screener who was looking at Arab Americans or South Asians. Can ethnic profiling make sense when terrorists wear so many different faces? Many people doubt it.

Muslim Terrorists May Come from All Over the World

During the last decade, most of the acts of terrorism directed at Americans and other Westerners were committed by young Muslim men. (An exception is the Irish Republican Army, from Northern Ireland, which has planted bombs in the United Kingdom.) Some argue that profiling young Muslim men is not a workable idea. If the police on New York City's subway system wanted to do such a thing, they would be looking for men from southern Europe, Latin America, and North Africa as well as the Middle East and South Asia, for starters. In addition, there are many African American Muslims.

The American-Arab Anti-Discrimination Committee's Hussein Ibish pointed out, "Muslims come from almost every society in the world. . . . One in five people is a Muslim." Even if the police focused on Arabs, Ibish said, they would have a difficult time recognizing them all. "Arabs could look like southern Europeans . . . like North Africans, like central and South Asians, [or] like Latin Americans. You can't tell if someone's Arab by looking at them."

Sergeant Peter DiDomenica, a member of the Massachusetts State Police, agrees. DiDomenica trains screeners at Logan Airport, in Boston, the departure point for two of the four commercial airplanes that terrorists used in the attacks of 9/11. "I don't think it's really possible," he said, "to identify what someone looks like who is of [the Muslim] faith." Security screeners at Logan Airport do not use ethnic profiling for routine screening. Any attempt to monitor people with roots in so many parts of the world, some argue, would require more time and attention than airport screeners have available.

Profiles Are Sometimes Incorrect

When, right after 9/11, some experienced intelligence officials wrote a memo advising law enforcement officers not to profile, they admitted that it is very tempting. "Tons of information is coming in from everywhere," one of the officials told the *Boston Globe*. "If you give people a profile, it helps [them] not be overwhelmed by the stream of information." They also make people feel safer.

But profiles have failed in the past, the officials pointed out. In the 1970s, the Secret Service, which protects the president of the United States, assumed that a person who wanted to assassinate the president would be a loner, almost certainly a man, and probably mentally ill. In 1975, Sara Jane Moore shattered that profile when she shot at President Gerald Ford.

Before September 11, one common profile of a would-be suicide terrorist was an uneducated teenager who was, again, a loner. The terrorists who brought Americans 9/11 did not fit that profile. They were older and better educated, but ready to give up everything for the religious fight they are waging against the West.

Behavior Is More Important than Appearance

The main reason the intelligence officials cautioned against profiling in their memo is that it distracts security and law enforcement officials from observing people's behavior, which they believe is much more important than someone's physical features. "Why are we in the situation we're in?" one of them asked a *Boston Globe* reporter. It wasn't really a question as far as he was concerned, and he answered it himself. "We were paying attention to a set of characteristics instead of a set of behaviors that launch an attack."

Nervousness is a red flag. Ressam's anxious behavior at the ferry terminal in Washington in 1999 attracted the attention of a customs official, for example. At Logan Airport, Sergeant DiDomenica trains airport security screeners to look for similar signs of stress. He explained why to a newscaster on National Public Radio: "An individual who is on some type of a mission would tend to feel some stress when they go through a screening process or . . . when they're in the presence of a law enforcement official," he said. "And that stress is not due to the person feeling guilty about what they're doing. . . . There is a stress created by a fear of failure or a fear of discovery."

At Logan, if a traveler is very anxious, a law enforcement official may talk with him to determine whether he is simply afraid to fly or worried about missing a business meeting. If the official still has concerns, he may have the person's luggage inspected and pat the person down.

Terrorist Organizations Can Work Around Ethnic Profiles

Some critics of ethnic profiling point out that terrorist organizations like Al Qaeda, which organized the 9/11 attacks, will recruit people who do not fit the standard profiles to go on terrorist missions. Richard Harris, a legal scholar and noted critic of racial and ethnic profiling, believes that the man commonly referred to as the "shoe bomber" was a good example.

On December 22, 2001, Richard Reid, a twenty-eight-year-old British citizen, was seated on an American Airlines jet flying from Paris to Miami. When he tried to ignite the explosives packed into one of his black suede high-top sneakers, eight passengers used their belts and earphone wires to tie him up and keep him still until the plane landed. This man, who nearly exploded the airplane, had family roots in Jamaica, far from the Middle East.

Al Qaeda's answer to the airport profile, Harris said, was "a non-Arab, non-Middle Easterner from England; a British citizen with a valid British passport and a bomb in his shoe." Random searches, Harris said, are an important security tactic because they are unpredictable.

Ethnic Profiling Discourages Arab Americans and Muslims from Sharing Intelligence

This is a variation of an argument against racial profiling directed at African Americans and Latinos. The state troopers who targeted minorities on the highways made some of them very distrustful of law enforcement officials. The same is true of Arab Americans, South Asians, and others who are repeatedly questioned and searched in airports and other public places where security is important. Someone who has valuable intelligence to share with law enforcement agents about a terrorist or a planned attack may hesitate if she is fearful or angry at the way she has been treated. Since intelligence is so crucial to fighting terrorism, it is best to avoid a tactic that antagonizes people.

Much Has Changed, and Much Remains the Same

Almost everyone feels less secure than he or she did before 9/11. A short ride on a subway can be a little different. On a train in Boston, next to an advertisement from one of the many local colleges, there may be a sign from the transit authority that reads, "See something? Say something," followed by a phone number. The "something" could be a package that seemed to belong to no one, or a person who looks very nervous and is sweating a lot. Either could mean there is a bomb nearby.

Some changes may depend on what you look like. The obvious example is flying. In airports from Miami to Los Angeles, seasoned travelers who never used to notice the strangers sharing a plane may be more wary now. They may even, unconsciously, look for faces like the nineteen Middle Eastern men who appeared in the newspapers over and over again right after September 11. Arab Americans, on the other hand, may become uneasy as they approach an airport screener. Will they be stopped, yet again, for "Flying while Arab"?

It has certainly become more difficult to answer one question in particular: Should law enforcement and security officials profile? It was so much easier to say "yes" or "no" before September 11. Some people have switched sides because of the awful possibility of another attack, as destructive or even worse. Others think ethnic profiling doesn't work well enough, and comes with a huge risk: the loss of racial and ethnic harmony in a land that has for centuries promised freedom to immigrants from all over the world.

Other things—good and bad—are still essentially the same. Most of our civil liberties are intact. Someone who strongly opposes some sections of the Patriot Act can write to her local newspaper. If she's lucky, she will see her letter in print. Certainly, the newspaper won't censor it. Her right of free speech is still protected by the First Amendment.

Even though the fight against terrorism occupies a lot of law enforcement attention, police officers continue to look for illegal drugs. That's a good thing, too. But in many parts of the country, African Americans are often pulled over for traffic stops. Most African Americans and many other Americans think that's a violation of the Fourth Amendment. And that's a bad thing.

7
The Future of Racial Profiling

The United States is a country with a lot of sunshine, even in rainy places like western Washington. Political commentators often use the word "sunshine" to mean "out in the open," and Americans are used to a very open society. Since 9/11, we have had to adjust to the fact that law enforcement now operates with more secrecy. People may be profiled without realizing it, and this is likely to continue in the future.

The Patriot Act has created some shade, or secrecy, where there was sunshine, in the hope of making the nation more secure. Though some of the controversial sections of the act were due to expire in 2005, the House and Senate both voted to make permanent most of the act's provisions. The act renewed a controversial provision that lets federal officials obtain "tangible items," such as business records, from libraries and bookstores, and even from doctors. One significant change *was* made: when a medical office, bookstore, library, or another business or organization receives a subpoena from the government for an individual's records, it can argue in court for the right to discuss this request publicly instead of keeping it secret. But it still has to give up the person's records.

Since these subpoenas are usually surrounded by secrecy, it is impossible to know whether they have been used to target Arab Americans, for example. And that makes the American-Arab Anti-Discrimination Committee uncomfortable.

Racial Profiling on the Roads

The state and local police who are collecting traffic stop data and sharing it with their communities are in a very real sense providing sunshine. They are letting the public know the extent of racial profiling in their departments.

Over a third of the states in the country are currently collecting traffic stop data to look for patterns of racial disparities in law enforcement. Those who oppose racial profiling hope this data collection will be a step toward eliminating it in those states. And they would like other states to do the same. Of course there are no guarantees.

On November 17, 2005, the American Civil Liberties Union issued a report on recent traffic stop data from Rhode Island. It found that African-American and Latino drivers were more likely to be searched than white drivers. The ACLU concluded there was no improvement since the previous study of Rhode Island's traffic stops, which was done in 2002. Researchers hope that other states and communities who are collecting data will see more positive results.

A Commissioner Who Wants the Streets of His Multicultural City Policed without Profiling

Ronnie Watson is the police commissioner of Cambridge, Massachusetts, a small city of about 100,000 people outside of Boston. The traffic stop data that the Cambridge Police Department collected in 2001–2002 showed that police officers were issuing a disproportionate number of tickets to African Americans. Watson, who is African American himself, is against profiling and is committed to eliminating racial disparities in law enforcement in his city. In addition to working with his own officers, Watson has helped train law enforcement agencies around Massachusetts to avoid racial profiling.

Among the minority populations in Cambridge, some are Muslim. Watson instructs his police force not to profile Muslim people, including the college students walking around the city's streets with large backpacks.

"When 9/11 happened," Watson said, "we were one of the few communities in Massachusetts that had a mosque. The number one priority in our city was to protect that mosque and the people that go to it from backlash [people wanting revenge]. We were able ensure that nothing happened to these people or the mosque." Watson added that his officers continue to monitor the Muslim house of worship, and he seems to take a personal interest and obvious pride in keeping it safe.

ZACHARIAS MOUSSAOUI IS A FRENCH CITIZEN WHO WAS SENTENCED TO LIFE IN PRISON IN 2006 FOR HIS ROLE IN THE 9/11 TERRORIST ATTACKS. MOUSSAOUI KNEW SOME OF THE HIJACKERS AND PLEADED GUILTY TO THE U.S. GOVERNMENT'S CHARGE OF CONSPIRACY.

Is Racial and Ethnic Profiling Here to Stay?

Opponents of racial profiling would like to see the day when police and security officials enforce the law without paying any attention to a person's race or ethnic background. Some of these opponents, however, don't really think that day will come. One scholar noted that our "real world" contains racial prejudice and also a disproportionate number of African-American criminals. For these reasons, among others, he believes police officers will continue to use racial profiling, even if they don't want to admit it.

In the fight against terrorists, security and law enforcement officials may never completely abandon ethnic profiling, either, especially those who work behind the scenes, gathering intelligence. Some journalists have never forgotten a serious incident that they believe came about because the FBI didn't want to be accused of using ethnic profiling itself.

Zacharias Moussaoui is a French citizen with family roots in Morocco. He was arrested on August 17, 2001, in Minnesota because of a problem with his passport. While he was in prison, FBI agents in Minnesota tried to get permission to search his belongings, but senior FBI officials would not permit the search. If the agents had examined his laptop computer before September 11, they would have discovered his connection with one of the key hijackers of the 9/11 attacks. Maybe that clue would have helped prevent the attacks. No one will know, but ethnic profiling is now officially part of the federal government's anti-terrorist tactics in special situations.

A Point of Agreement

Racial and ethnic profiling is a controversial issue. There are many aspects of this law enforcement tactic that provoke debates. But responsible professionals and citizens do agree on one thing: For as long as profiling is with us, it should be done respectfully, and by professionals. Profiling is supposed to be a technique, not a way of life. The United States has long been a mosaic of many peoples and cultures. That is something to celebrate.

Notes

Introduction

p. 9, "Racial Profiling within Law Enforcement Agencies."
http: //purl.access.gpo.gov/GPO/LPS15529 (Accessed
September 9, 2005)

p. 9, Heumann, Milton, and Lance Cassak. *Good Cop, Bad
Cop: Racial Profiling and Competing Views of Justice*,
Studies in Crime and Punishment, 10. New York: Peter
Lang, 2003, p. 117.

p. 9, Cleary, Jim, "Racial Profiling Studies in Law
Enforcement: Issues and Methodology," Minnesota House
of Representatives p. 5. http://www.house.leg.state.mn.
us/hrd/
pubs/raceprof.pdf

p. 10, Kennedy, Randall, "Suspect Policy," *The New Republic*,
September 13 and 20, 1999, p. 35.

p. 10, Goldberg, Jeffrey, "The Color of Suspicion," *New York
Times*, p. 5. http://query.nytimes.com

p. 10, Hamilton, Anita, and Peter Bailey, "Recharging the
Mission: The NAACP Is Looking for a New Leader." *Time*,
January 17, 2005. http://elibrary.bigchalk.com

p. 11, Quoted in Heumann and Cassak. *Good Cop, Bad Cop*,
p. 102.

p. 11, Kennedy. "Suspect Policy," p. 33.

p. 11, Heumann and Cassak. *Good Cop, Bad Cop*, p.191,
note 5.

p. 12, Heumann and Cassak. *Good Cop, Bad Cop*, p. 4.

p. 13, "Face to Face," http://www.itvs.org/facetoface/intro.
html (Accessed September 30, 2005)

Chapter 1
p. 14, "Face to Face," http://www.itvs.org/facetoface/intro.
html (Accessed September 30, 2005)
p. 15, Wu, Frank H., "Profiling in the Wake of September 11:
The Precedent of the Japanese Internment," in *Civil
Liberties vs. National Security in a Post-9/11 World,* ed.
M. Katherine B. Darmer, Robert M. Barid, and Stuart E.
Rosenbaum. Amherst, NY: Prometheus Books, 2004, p.
147.
p. 17, Norton, Mary Beth, et al., *A People and a Nation: A
History of the United States,* 3rd ed. Boston: Houghton
Mifflin, p. 783.
p. 17, Muller, Eric L., "Inference or Impact? Racial Profiling
and Internment's True Legacy," *Ohio State Journal of
Criminal Law,* Spring 2004, p. 110.
p. 17, "All Things Considered," National Public Radio,
November 26, 2002.
p. 17, Malkin, Michelle. *In Defense of Internment:
The Case for 'Racial Profiling' in World War II and the War
on Terror.* Washington, DC: Regnery Publishing, p. 66.
p. 18, Malkin. *In Defense of Internment,* p. 70.
p. 18, Muller, "Inference or Impact?" p. 111.
p. 19, Wu, "Profiling in the Wake of September 11," p. 149.
p. 19, "Face to Face," http://www.itvs.org/facetoface/intro.
html (Accessed September 30, 2005)
p. 19, "American Refugees: The Japanese-American
Relocation," American Friends Service Committee,
http://www.absc.org/about/hist/2002/japanam.htm
(Accessed March 26, 2006)
p. 20, *All Things Considered,* National Public Radio,
November 26, 2002.
p. 21, Muller, "Inference or Impact?" p. 113.
p. 21, "All Things Considered," National Public Radio,
November 26, 2002.
p. 23, Quoted in Malkin. *In Defense of Internment,* p. 114.
p. 24, Malkin. *In Defense of Internment,* p. 114.
p. 24, Muller, "Inference or Impact?" pp. 115–116.
p. 24, Muller, "Inference or Impact?" p. 118.
p. 25, "Face to Face," http://www.itvs.org/facetoface/intro.
html (Accessed September 30, 2005)

Chapter 2

p. 27, *Bombing of America*, NOVA, March 25, 1997. http://www.pbs.org/wgbh/nova/transcripts/2310tbomb.html, p. 11. (Accessed September 30, 2005)

p. 27, "Remembering the Former Mad Bomber," *All Things Considered*, National Public Radio, November 3, 2005.

p. 27, DeNevi, Don, and John H. Campbell. *Into the Minds of Madmen*. Amherst, NY: Prometheus Books, 2004, p. 62.

p. 29, DeNevi and Campbell. *Into the Minds of Madmen*.

p. 30, "Significant Terrorist Incidents, 1961–2003: A Brief Chronology," http://www.state.gov/r/pa/ho/pubs/fs/5902.htm (Accessed September 30, 2005)

p. 30, Hough, Robert, "Unusual Suspect: Thirty Years After He Robbed a Bank and Hijacked a Plane to Cuba, Patrick Critton was Finally Busted," *Toronto Life*, http://www.elibrary.bigchalk.com'libweb/elib/do/document?set=search&groupid=1&requestid=1 (Accessed June 23, 2005)

p. 31, "Aviation Security," U.S. Centennial of Flight Commission, http://www.centennialofflight.gov/essay/Government_Role/security/POL 18.htm (Accessed November 4, 2005), and David A. Harris. *Profiles in Injustice: Why Racial Profiling Cannot Work*, New York: The New Press, 2002, pp. 17–18.

p. 32, Heumann, Milton, and Lance Cassak. *Good Cop, Bad Cop: Racial Profiling and Competing Views of Justice*, Studies in Crime and Punishment, 10. New York: Peter Lang, p. 33.

p. 32, Heumann and Cassak. *Good Cop, Bad Cop*, p. 25.

p. 35, "DEA History Book, 1975-1980," DEA, http://www.usdoj.gov/dea/pubs/history/deahistory01.htm (Accessed November 6, 2005)

p. 35, Heumann and Cassak. *Good Cop, Bad Cop*, p. 43.

p. 36, Heumann and Cassak. *Good Cop, Bad Cop*, p. 45.

p. 36, Heumann and Cassak. *Good Cop, Bad Cop*, p. 47 and 50.

p. 37, Harris. *Profiles in Injustice*, p. 22.

p. 39, Heumann and Cassak. *Good Cop, Bad Cop*, pp. 80-85.

p. 40, "Anti-Drug Interdiction Efforts: Donnie Marshall, Congressional Testimony, 9/16/98." http://www.elibrary.bigchalk.com. (Accessed June 23, 2005)

Chapter 3

p. 43, Most, Doug, "Shot Through the Heart," *Sports Illustrated*, July 10, 2000. http://www.elibrary.bigchalk.com (Accessed September 5, 2005)

p. 45, Milton Heumann and Lance Cassak. *Good Cop, Bad Cop: Racial Profiling and Competing Views of Justice*, Studies in Crime and Punishment 10, New York: Peter Lang, 2003, p. 74.

p. 45, Heumann and Cassak. *Good Cop, Bad Cop*, p. 93.

p. 46, Harris, David, " 'Driving While Black' and All Other Traffic Offenses: The Supreme Court and Pretextual Traffic Stops," *Journal of Criminal Law and Criminology* 82, no. 2 (Winter 1997), p. 570.

p. 46, Harris, David. *Profiles in Injustice: Why Racial Profiling Cannot Work*, New York: The New Press, p. 61.

p. 47, Lamberth, John, "Driving While Black: A Statistician Proves That Prejudice Still Rules the Road," *Washington Post*, August 16, 1998, p. C1.

p. 48, Fletcher, Michael A., "Driven to Extremes: Black Men Take Steps to Avoid Stops," *Washington Post*, March 29, 1996.

p. 48, "History of Racial Profiling Analysis," Racial Profiling Data Collection Resource Center at Northeastern University, http://www.racialprofilinganalysis.neu.edu (Accessed September 30, 2005)

p. 48, "Special Report II: Racial Profiling—Overcoming the Perception of Racial Profiling," *Law and Order*, April 1, 2001. http://www.elibrary.bigchalk.com (Accessed September 30, 2005)

p. 49, "History of Racial Profiling Analysis," Racial Profiling Data Collection Resource Center at Northeastern University, http://www.racialprofilinganalysis.neu.edu (Accessed September 30, 2005)

p. 49, "Background and Current Data Collection Efforts," Racial Profiling Data Collection Resource Center at Northeastern University, http://www.racialprofilinganaly sis.neu.edu (Accessed September 30, 2005)

p. 50–51, Telephone interview with Jack McDevitt, August 11, 2005.

p. 52, McDevitt, Jack, and Lisa Bailey, "Looking Deeper at Racial Profiling," *Boston Globe*, August 2, 2003, p. A19.

p. 53, Levenson, Michael. "State on Hunt for Racial Profiling—Police Report Adds Context to Road Stops," *Boston Globe*, July 5, 2005, p. A1.

p. 54, Telephone interview with Ronnie Watson, September 1, 2005.

p. 54, Frederickson, Darin, and Raymond Siljander. *Racial Profiling: Eliminating the Confusion between Racial and Criminal Profiling and Clarifying What Constitutes Unfair*

Discrimination and Persecution. Springfield, IL: Charles C. Thomas Publishing, 2002, pp. 65 and 67.

Chapter 4

p. 55, Meeks, Kenneth. *Driving While Black: What to Do If You Are the Victim of Racial Profiling.* New York: Broadway Books, 2000, pp. 65–66.

p. 57, Jeffrey Goldberg, "The Color of Suspicion," *New York Times Magazine,* June 20, 1999. http://query.nytimes.com/ search /restricted, p. 5. (Accessed July 21, 2005)

p. 57, Frederickson, Darin, and Raymond Siljander. *Racial Profiling: Eliminating the Confusion between Racial and Criminal Profiling and Clarifying What Constitutes Unfair Discrimination and Persecution.* Springfield, IL: Charles C. Thomas Publishing, 2002, p. 22.

p. 57, Quoted in Milton Heumann and Lance Cassak. *Good Cop, Bad Cop: Racial Profiling and Competing Views of Justice,* Studies in Crime and Punishment. 10, New York: Peter Lang, 2003, p. 112.

pp. 57–58, Frederickson and Siljander, *Racial Profiling,* p.50.

p. 58, Goldberg, Jeffrey, "The Color of Suspicion," *New York Times Magazine,* June 20, 1999. http://query.nytimes.com/ search/restricted, p. 6. (Accessed July 21, 2005)

p. 58, Goldberg, *The Color of Suspicion,* pp. 1–2.

p. 59, Cleary, Jim, "Racial Profiling Studies in Law Enforcement: Issues and Methodology," Minnesota House of Representatives, http://www.house.leg.state.mn.us/hrd/ pubs/raceprof.pdf, p. 20 (Accessed July 21, 2005)

p. 59, Cloud, John, "What's Race Got to Do with It?", *Time,* July 22, 2001. http://www.time.com/time/covers/11010107 30/cover.html, pp. 2, 9–10. (Accessed July 21, 2005)

pp. 59–60, Stuntz, William J., "Local Policing After the Terror," *Yale Law Journal* 111 (June 2002) p. 2179.

p. 60, Rasinya, Dean, "Letters," *New York Times Magazine,* July 11, 1999, p. 6.

p. 61, Harcourt, Bernard, "Rethinking Racial Profiling: A Critique of the Economics, Civil Liberties, and Constitutional Literature, and of Criminal Profiling More Generally," *University of Chicago Law Review* 71 (Fall 2004), p. 1283.

p. 62, Quoted in Heumann and Cassak. *Good Cop, Bad Cop,* p. 105.

p. 62, Meeks, *Driving While Black,* p. 57.

p. 63, Cooper, Michael, "Woman Wins 1992 Lawsuit Charging Race Profiling," *New York Times,* p. A19.

pp. 63–64, Kennedy, Randall, "Suspect Policy," *The New Republic*, September 13 and 20, 1999, p. 33.

pp. 64-65, Glasser, Ira, "Letters," *New York Times Magazine*, July 11, 1999, p. 6.

p. 65, "Who's a Looter? In Storm's Aftermath Pictures Kick Up a Different Kind of Tempest, *New York Times*, September 5, 2005. http://www.infoweb.newsbank.com (Accessed July 21, 2005)

p. 65, Harcourt, "Rethinking Racial Profiling," p. 1376.

p. 66, Kennedy, "Suspect Policy," p. 34.

Chapter 5

p. 68, "The Bill of Rights: A Transcription," U.S. National Archives and Records Administration. http://www.archives. gov/national-archives-experience/charters/bill_of_rights_ transcript.html (November 27, 2005)

p. 69, 323 U.S. 214 (1944)

p. 70, Anonymous, "Civil Liberties Hero, Fred Korematsu, Remembered," *Peacework*, June 1, 2005, from http://www. elibrary.bigchalk.com (Accessed November 27, 2005)

p. 71, Heumann, Milton, and Lance Cassak. *Good Cop, Bad Cop: Racial Profiling and Competing Views of Justice*, Studies in Crime and Punishment, 10. New York: Peter Lang, 2003, p.19.

p. 71, *Terry v. Ohio*, 392 U.S. 1 (1968).

p. 72, "The Bill of Rights: A Transcription," U.S. National Archives and Records Administration. http://www.archives. gov/national-archives-experience/charters/bill_of_rights_ transcript.html (Accessed November 27, 2005)

p. 74, *United States v. Martinez-Fuerte*, 428 U.S. 543, 563 (1976).

p. 74, Quoted in Heumann and Cassak. *Good Cop, Bad Cop*, p. 126.

p. 75, *United States v. Sokolow*, 490 U.S. 1 (1989).

p. 75, Quoted in David A. Harris, *Profiles in Injustice: Why Racial Profiling Cannot Work*. New York: The New Press, p. 20.

p. 76, Quoted in Heumann and Cassak. *Good Cop, Bad Cop*, p. 63.

p. 77, *Whren v. United States*, 517 U.S. 806(1996).

p. 78, Heumann and Cassak. *Good Cop, Bad Cop*, p. 132.

p. 78, Harris, David A., " 'Driving While Black' and All Other Traffic Offenses: The Supreme Court and Pretextual Traffic Stops," *The Journal of Criminal Law and Criminology* 87, no. 2 (Winter 1997), p. 558.

p. 78, 734 A. 2d 350 (N.J. Super. Ct. Law. Div. 1996)
p. 79, Heumann and Cassak.*Good Cop, Bad Cop,*
pp. 135–136.

Chapter 6
p. 82, Verhovek, Sam Howe, with Tim Weiner, "Man Seized
with Bomb Parts at Border Spurs U.S. Inquiry," *New York
Times*, p. A15, and *Newsnight with Aaron Brown*, July 28,
2005, http://www.CNN.com (Accessed September 6, 2005)
p. 83, Harris, David, "Racial Profiling Revisited: Just
Common Sense in the Fight Against Terror," in *Civil
Liberties vs. National Security in a Post-9/11 World*, ed. M.
Katherine B. Darmer, Robert M. Barid, and Stuart E.
Rosenbaum. Amherst, NY: Prometheus Books, 2004,
p. 163.
p. 84, Cole, David. *Enemy Aliens: Double Standards and
Constitutional Freedoms in the War on Terrorism*, New
York: The New Press, 2003, p. 47.
p. 84, Conan, Neil, "The Experience of Arab-Americans Since
9/11," *Talk of the Nation*, March 11, 2003.
p. 84, Greenhouse, Linda, "In New York Visit, O'Connor
Foresees Limits on Freedom," *New York Times*, p. 5.
p. 87, "Resolution on the USA Patriot Act and Related
Measures That Infringe on the Rights of Library Users,"
American Library Association, http://www.ala.org
(September 23, 2005)
p. 88, "Update on ADC's Challenge to the USA Patriot Act,"
November 3, 2003, ADC: American-Arab Anti-
Discrimination Committee, http://www.adc.org (Accessed
August 22, 2005)
p. 89, Butterfield, Fox, "Police are Split On Questioning of
Mideast Men," *New York Times*, November 22, 2001, p. 1.
p. 90, Lichtblau, Eric, "Bush Issues Racial Profiling Ban But
Exempts Security Inquiries," *New York Times*, June 18,
2003, p. 1.
p. 93, Sperry, Paul, "It's the Age of Terror: What Would You
Do?", *New York Times*, July 28, 2005, p. 25.
p. 93, Quoted in Milton Heumann and Lance Cassak. *Good
Cop, Bad Cop: Racial Profiling and Competing Views of
Justice*, Studies in Crime and Punishment, 10, New York:
Peter Lang, 2003, p. 177.
p. 93, Taylor Jr., Stuart, "The Skies Won't Be Safe Until We
Use Commonsense Profiling," in *Civil Liberties vs. National
Security in a Post-9/11 World*, ed. M. Katherine B.
Darmer, Robert M. Barid, and Stuart E. Rosenbaum.
Amherst, NY: Prometheus Books, 2004, p. 159.

p. 94, Malti-Douglas, Fedwa, "Let Them Profile Me," *New York Times*, February 6, 2002, p. 21.

p. 94, Schuck, Peter, "A Case for Profiling," January 27, 2002, Yale Law School Web site, http://www. law.yale.edu/outside/tm./Ppublic_Affairs (Accessed July 21, 2005)

p. 95, Kristof, Nicholas D., "Liberal Reality Check," *New York Times*, May 31, 2002, p. 23.

p. 96, *Newsnight with Aaron Brown*, July 28, 2005, http://www.cnn.com (Accessed September 6, 2005)

p. 96, *Weekend Edition* with Scott Simon, "Counterterrorism: Training Transportation Screeners," July 30, 2005, http://npr.org (Accessed August 21, 2005)

p. 97, Dedman, Bill, "Memo Warns Against Use of Profiling As a Defense," *Boston Globe*, October 12, 2001, p. A27.

p. 98, Dedman, "Memo Warns Against Use of Profiling," p. A27.

p. 99, Harris, David, "Racial Profiling Revisited: Just Common Sense in the Fight Against Terror," in *Civil Liberties vs. National Security in a Post-9/11 World*, ed. M. Katherine B. Darmer, Robert M. Barid, and Stuart E. Rosenbaum, p. 173.

Chapter 7

p. 101, "Bush Signs Renewal of Patriot Act Into Law," *Associated Press*, March 9, 2006.

p. 102, "ACLU Report Uncovers Racial Profiling and Poor Police Work in Rhode Island," Amercian Civil Liberties Union, November 17, 2005, http://www.aclu.org/racial profiling (Accessed September 5, 2005)

p. 103, Personal conversation, September 1, 2005.

p. 104, Heumann, Milton, and Lance Cassak. *Good Cop, Bad Cop: Racial Profiling and Competing Views of Justice*, Studies in Crime and Punishment, p. 160.

p. 105, Heumann and Cassak. *Good Cop, Bad Cop*, pp. 170–171.

Further Information

Books

Bumgarner, Jeffrey B. *Profiling and Criminal Justice in America*, Contemporary World Issues. Santa Barbara, CA: ABC-CLIO, 2004.

Harris, David A. *Profiles in Injustice: Why Racial Profiling Cannot Work*. New York: The New Press, 2002.

Houston, James D., and Jeanne Wakatsuki Houston. *Farewell to Manzanar: A True Story of Japanese American Experience During and After the World War II Internment*. Boston: Houghton Mifflin, 2002.

Lee, Frances Graham. *Equal Protection: Rights and Liberties Under the Law*. Santa Barbara, CA: ABC-CLIO, 2004.

Magnum Photographers. *New York: September 11*. New York: Power Books, 2001.

Web Sites

American-Arab Anti-Discrimination Committee
http://www.adc.org

American Civil Liberties Union
http://www.aclu.org/racialjustice/racialprofiling/index.html

Amnesty International USA: Racial Profiling
http://www.amnestyusa.org/racial_profiling/report/

Arab American Institute
http://www.aaiusa.org

Children of the Camps
http://www.children-of-the-camps.org/

Core Documents of U.S. Democracy,
http://www.gpoaccess.gov/coredocs.html

Face to Face: Stories from the Aftermath of Infamy
http://www.itvs.org/facetoface/intro.html

National Association for the Advancement of Colored People
http://www.naacp.org

Newshour Extra: Life After 9/11
http://www.pbs.org/newshour/extra/features/after911/

Of Civil Wrongs and Rights: The Fred Korematsu Story
http://www.pbs.org/pov/pov2001/ofcivilwrongsandrights/
resources.html

Police Foundation
http://www.policefoundation.org

U.S. Department of Justice
http://www.usdoj.gov

U.S. Drug Enforcement Administration: DEA History Book
http://www.usdoj.gov/dea/pubs/history/index.html

World Trade Center
http://www.greatbuildings.com/buildings/World_Trade_
Center.html

Bibliography

Books

Cole, David. *Enemy Aliens: Double Standards and Constitutional Freedoms in the War on Terrorism.* New York: The New Press, 2003.

Darmer, M. Katherine B., Robert M. Barid, and Stuart E. Rosenbaum, eds. *Civil Liberties vs. National Security in a Post-9/11 World.* Amherst, NY: Prometheus Books, 2004.

DeNevi, Don, and John H. Campbell. *Into the Minds of Madmen.* Amherst, NY: Prometheus Books, 2004.

Frederickson, Darin, and Raymond Siljander. *Racial Profiling: Eliminating the Confusion between Racial and Criminal Profiling and Clarifying What Constitutes Unfair Discrimination and Persecution.* Springfield, IL: Charles C. Thomas Publishing, 2002.

Harris, David A. *Profiles in Injustice: Why Racial Profiling Cannot Work.* New York: The New Press, 2002

Heumann, Milton, and Lance Cassak. *Good Cop, Bad Cop: Racial Profiling and Competing Views of Justice*, Studies in Crime and Punishment, 10. New York: Peter Lang, 2003.

Malkin, Michelle. *In Defense of Internment: The Case for 'Racial Profiling' in World War II and the War on Terror.* Washington, DC: Regnery Publishing, 2004.

Meeks, Kenneth. *Driving While Black: What to Do If You Are the Victim of Racial Profiling.* New York: Broadway Books, 2000.

O'Reilly, James T. *Police Traffic Stops and Racial Profiling: Resolving Management, Labor, and Civil Rights Conflicts.* Springfield, IL: Charles C. Thomas, 2002.

Newspapers and Periodicals

Butterfield, Fox. "Police are Split On Questioning of Mideast Men," *New York Times,* November 22, 2001.

Cloud, John. "What's Race Got to Do with It?" *Time,* July 22, 2001.

Goldberg, Jeffrey. "The Color of Suspicion," *New York Times Magazine,* June 20, 1999.

Greenhouse, Linda. "In New York Visit, O'Connor Foresees Limits on Freedom," *New York Times,* September 29, 2001, p. 5.

Harris, David. " 'Driving While Black' and All Other Traffic Offenses: The Supreme Court and Pretextual Traffic Stops," *Journal of Criminal Law and Criminology* 82, no. 2 (Winter 1997).

Harcourt, Bernard. "Rethinking Racial Profiling: A Critique of the Economics, Civil Liberties, and Constitutional Literature, and of Criminal Profiling More Generally," *University of Chicago Law Review,* 71 (Fall 2004).

Kennedy, Randall. "Suspect Policy," *The New Republic,* September 13 and 20, 1999.

Lamberth, John. "Driving While Black: A Statistician Proves That Prejudice Still Rules the Road," *Washington Post,* August 16, 1998.

Levenson, Michael. "State on Hunt for Racial Profiling—Police Report Adds Context to Road Stops," *Boston Globe,* July 5, 2005.

Lichtblau, Eric. "Bush Issues Racial Profiling Ban But Exempts Security Inquiries," *New York Times*, June 18, 2003.

Most, Doug. "Shot Through the Heart," *Sports Illustrated*, July 10, 2000.

Muller, Eric L. "Inference or Impact? Racial Profiling and Internment's True Legacy," *Ohio State Journal of Criminal Law*, Spring 2004.

Ralli, Tania. "Who's a Looter? In Storm's Aftermath Pictures Kick Up a Different Kind of Tempest, *New York Times*, September 5, 2005.

Stuntz, William J. "Local Policing After the Terror," *Yale Law Journal* 111, (June 2002).

Wiseman, Jonathan, "Congress Arrives at a Deal on Patriot Act," *Washington Post*, November 17, 2005.

Index

Page numbers in **boldface** are illustrations.

About the Author

Deborah Kops has written more than a dozen books for young people on a variety of subjects in the fields of history and natural science. She edited scholarly books on criminal justice and American history at Northeastern University Press, and then edited nonfiction childrens' books at Blackbirch Press. She now writes from her home in Greater Boston, which she shares with her husband and son. *Racial Profiling* is her first book for Benchmark Books.